Seven Sūrahs

for the classroom

Junior Level · General

Arabic Text, Translations, Explanations & Vocabulary

Compilation: Abidullah Ghazi
Ph.D. History of Religion, Harvard University

Translations: Abdullah Yusuf Ali and
Muhammad Marmaduke Pickthal
Rendered in Modern English

Explanations: Abdullah Yusuf Ali
Revised and Abridged

IQRA' International Educational Foundation, Chicago

Part of a Comprehensive and Systematic Program of Islamic Studies

A Textbook for
Qur'anic Studies
Junior Level

Chief Program Editors
Dr. Abidullah al-Ansari Ghazi
(Ph.D., History of Religion
Harvard University)

Tasneema Ghazi
(Ph.D., Curriculum-Reading
University of Minnesota)

Religious Review
Maulana Shu'aib ud-Din Qutub
(Faḍil Dar ul-Ulum, Karachi)

Bassam Helwani

Language Editing
Hina Akhtar
(B.S. Zoology, University of Maryland
M.Ed. Pending Loyola)

Huda Quraishi
(B.Sc., University of Illinois, Chicago)

English Typesetting
Shaista N. Ali
(M.A. Mass Communications, Karachi
University, Pakistan)

Mahlaqa Patel
(B.Sc., University of Illinois, Chicago)

Arabic Typesetting
Randa Zaiter
(B.S. Social Science, University of Lebanon)

Cover Design
Kathryn Heimberger
(American Academy of Art)

Printed in the USA

Library of Congress Catalog Card Number 96-079298
ISBN # 1-56316-114-1

Table of Contents

بِسْمِ اللّٰهِ الرَّحْمٰنِ الرَّحِيْمِ

SEVEN SŪRAHS

IQRA'S NOTE: FOR PARENTS, TEACHERS AND READERS

IQRA' International Educational Foundation is pleased to offer *Seven Sūrahs* as a textbook at the junior level and as a Qur'ānic reading book for the general public.

All the *Suwar* in this volume have their own special importance, and are recited more frequently than others. They cover almost all of the important themes of the Qur'ān: *Tawḥīd* (The Oneness of Allāh ﷻ), *Risālah* (Prophethood), *Al-'Ākhirah,* (the Hereafter), establishment of the *Qiyāmah,* (The Day of Judgement), the pleasure of *Jannah,* and the ordeals of *Jahannam*. The selected *Suwar* enjoin such virtues as faith, patience, perseverance, trust, unity, generosity, struggle and honesty. They condemn disbelief, debauchery, falsehood, scandal, oppression and arrogance. These were the teachings of the Qur'ān which, under the guidance of the Prophet ﷺ, inspired the *Ṣaḥābah* ؓ and prepared them to be the noblest models of *Akhlāq* for all time to come.

This textbook is a part of IQRA'*s Comprehensive and Systematic Program of Islamic Studies,* which covers ten subjects and encompasses four levels: *pre-school, elementary, junior* and *senior*.

Division of the volume and lesson plan: Each Surah starts with an introduction and is divided into several *Rukū'*. `Each *Rukū'* (section) is treated as one complete lesson which must be covered in two or more days. Each *Rukū'* contains, ***Arabic text, two translations*** (`Abdullāh Yūsuf `Ali and M. M. Pickthal)***, An Explanation, Important Points to Learn and Reflect Upon, Glossary Words and a complete Vocabulary of Arabic Text***. (Each part of the lesson plan requires some further explanation.)

Transliteration: In transliterating, we followed the Library of Congress system with a few modifications (See Appendix I). We have followed the phonetic method to facilitate reading. The Arabic definite article *(al)* often assimilates its initial (a) in speech; while in writing, it does appear. Following the phonetic scheme, we have written it in transliteration within parenthesis. A letter appearing in the text but falling silent after the *'Āyah* is also shown in the vocabulary section within parenthesis. In transliterating the *Sūrah,* we have followed only the phonetic sound (as it must be pronounced before the *'Āyah*). Before or after the consonant letter of the *'Āyah,* the *ḥarakāt* (*`I`rāb*) do appear in parenthesis, but they are not read. For example:

1:1. *Rabbi al-`ālamīna* is written as *Rabbi-(a)l-`ālamīn(a)* and read as *Rabbi-l-`ālamīn.*
114:1. *Bi-Rabbi an-nāsi* is written as *Bi-Rabbi-(a)n-nās(i)* and read as *Bi-Rabbi-n-nās.*
Fi Al-Qur'āni al-Karīmi is transliterated as *fi-(a)l-Qur'āni-(a)l-Karīm(i) and read as fi-l-Qur'āni-l-Karīm.*

We have followed the phonetic rule in the usage of *Shamsī* (Sun) letters for example:

1:1 *Al-Raḥmāni Al-Raḥīmi* is transliterated as *Ar-Raḥmāni-(a)r-Raḥīm(i)* and read as *Ar-Raḥmāni-r-Raḥīm.*
114:1 *'Ilāhi al-nāsi* is transliterated as *'Ilāhi-(a)n-nās(i)* and read as *Ilāhi-n-nās.*

The entire IQRA' program is designed to teach students the reading and understanding of Qur'ānic Arabic. Therefore, we are not including the transliteration of the *Suwar* in this volume, since we expect our students to be proficient in the reading of the Arabic language by now.

Translations: We have provided two major translations side by side. The first translation is by `Abdullāh Yūsuf `Alī, and the second is by Muhammad Marmaduke Pickthal. A student will greatly benefit in understanding the Qur'ān by these two prominent scholars. Additionally, he/she will also understand the difficulties of translating Arabic text. These original translations in Old English are rendered into modern English, without tampering with the text at all. We have also used more accepted Islamic terminology (e.g. *Allāh* for God, *Messenger* for Apostle, etc.). We have, however, provided key Arabic terms next to the translation and the meaning of difficult words within parenthesis{}.

Commentary: For this volume, we have used the abbreviated and revised version of the commentary of Abdullah Yusuf `Alī and have tried to remain faithful to his understanding of the text. Certain points have been explained further and the compiler has added to `Alī's commentary in some places denoted by parenthesis and his initials {AG}.

Important Points to Learn and Reflect Upon: Each *Rukū'* ends with a section entitled *Important Points to Learn and Reflect Upon* and recaptures the central theme of that section in three brief points.

Glossary Words: The Glossary lists Arabic terms and difficult English words. Arabic words are explained in the "vocabulary," and must receive special attention.

Vocabulary: The meaning of every word in each *Sūrah* is provided at the end of each section. It will greatly enhance the student's understanding of the Qur'ānic text, and will aid in his/her learning of the Arabic language.

Workbooks: The workbooks, based on the pattern of our familiar *Sīrah Program,* and other popular textbooks, are under publication. Their aim is to provide reinforcement, develop educational skills, and provide additional practice.

This work is part of IQRA's pioneering efforts to introduce the meaning and message of the Qur'ān at every level. We pray to Allāh ﷻ that He accept this effort, and make it useful to all seekers of the truth, as contained in the final revelation: the Qur'ān.

We are thankful to Allāh ﷻ for the great popularity of ***Juz' `Amma: 30, Volume 1 (From An-Nās: 114 to Ash-Shams: 89 with Sūrah Al-Fātiḥah: 1) and Juz' `Amma: 30, Volume 2 (From Al-Balad: 90 to An-Naba':78).*** Since then, the demand to follow this scheme for the entire Qur'ān has increased. This textbook is one more step in that direction. We are pleased to inform you that we have already initiated the Qur'ān project, and have thus far completed the first three *Ajzā',* namely: *Juz' Alif Lām Mīm:* 1, *Sa-Yaqūl:* 2 and *Tilka Ar-Rusul:* 3. These textbooks also cover a study of *Sūrah al-Fātiḥah* and *Al-Baqarah,* and part of *Āl `Imrān*. We are recommending these textbooks for the Senior level.

As concerned parents and teachers, we urge you to support this pioneering educational endeavor through your *Du`ā',* advice and monetary contributions. We shall appreciate your opinion and comments to help us improve upon the revised edition.

Chief Editors
7450 Skokie Boulevard
Skokie, IL 60076

Jumu'ah, 23 Rabī' al-Awwal 1417 H
Friday, 9 August, 1996

SPECIAL NOTE: This first edition of *Seven Surahs* is being published for **opinion, review and field-testing**. We request you to kindly offer your input so that we can incorporate it in our revised and final version. *Jazāk Allāh.*

Section 1: 1-7

سُورَةُ الفَاتِحَة ١

SŪRAH AL-FĀTIḤAH 1:1-7

The Opening Chapter / The Opening

Name: This *Sūrah* is named *Al-Fātiḥah* because of its subject-matter. *Fātiḥah* is that which opens a subject, a book or any other thing. In other words, *Al-Fātiḥah* is a kind of preface to the Qur'ān. It is also known as the *'Umm al-Kitāb*, the "Mother of the Book."

Period of Revelation: It is one of the earliest revelations to the Holy Prophet ﷺ. We learn from authentic Traditions that it was the first complete *Sūrah* revealed to Rasūlullāh ﷺ.

Theme: This is the most important *Sūrah* of the Qur'ān. Rasūlullāh ﷺ said: "Such an important *Sūrah* as this was not sent down to any other prophet." This *Sūrah* is, in fact, a prayer which Allāh ﷾ has provided for all those who wish to approach Him through the *Ṣalāh*, to create a relationship with Him and to receive guidance from His book, the Qur'ān.

This *Sūrah* creates a strong desire in the heart of the sincere reader to seek guidance and help from Allāh ﷾, Who alone can grant this guidance. Thus, *Al-Fātiḥah* teaches that the best thing we can do for ourselves is to completely depend upon Allāh ﷾, *Rabb al-'Ālamīn*, the Lord of the Worlds, and the best thing to ask from Him is guidance to the Straight Path.

If *Al-Fātiḥah* is a prayer to Allāh ﷾ for the guidance, the Qur'ān is the answer to that prayer from Allāh ﷾. This *Sūrah* is recited in each *Raka`ah* (unit) of the ritual prayer.

ARABIC TEXT

بِسْمِ ٱللَّهِ ٱلرَّحْمَٰنِ ٱلرَّحِيمِ ﴿١﴾

ٱلْحَمْدُ لِلَّهِ رَبِّ ٱلْعَٰلَمِينَ ﴿٢﴾

ٱلرَّحْمَٰنِ ٱلرَّحِيمِ ﴿٣﴾ مَٰلِكِ يَوْمِ ٱلدِّينِ ﴿٤﴾

إِيَّاكَ نَعْبُدُ وَإِيَّاكَ نَسْتَعِينُ ﴿٥﴾ ٱهْدِنَا

ٱلصِّرَٰطَ ٱلْمُسْتَقِيمَ ﴿٦﴾ صِرَٰطَ ٱلَّذِينَ أَنْعَمْتَ

عَلَيْهِمْ غَيْرِ ٱلْمَغْضُوبِ عَلَيْهِمْ

وَلَا ٱلضَّآلِّينَ ﴿٧﴾

TRANSLATIONS

1. In the name of Allāh, Most Gracious, Most Merciful.
2. Praise be to Allāh, the Cherisher and Sustainer of the Worlds.
3. Most Gracious, Most Merciful.
4. Master of the Day of Judgement.
5. You do we worship, and Your aid we seek.
6. Show us the straight way.
7. The way of those on whom You have bestowed Your Grace; Those whose (portion) is not wrath, and who go not astray.
(A. Y. Ali)

1. In the name of Allāh, the Beneficent, the Merciful.
2. Praise be to Allāh, Lord of the Worlds:
3. The Beneficent, the Merciful:
4. Owner of the Day of Judgement.
5. You (alone) we worship; You alone we ask for help.
6. Show us the straight path:
7. The path of those whom You have favored; Not (the path) of those who earn Your anger, nor of those who go astray.
(M. M. Pickthal)

EXPLANATION (A. Y. Ali, revised)

1: The Arabic words *Raḥmān* and *Raḥīm,* translated as 'Most Gracious' and 'Most Merciful,' have their root in the Arabic term *Raḥīma,* meaning "to have mercy." Both words are intensive forms of "*Raḥīma*" and express the strength and depth of God's Mercy. Mercy may imply kindness, patience, sympathy and forgiveness, all of which a human needs, and which God, the Most Merciful, bestows in abundant measure. However, there is a mercy that is always present, even before the need arises. The Grace of Allāh ﷻ is ever-watchful of all His creatures, protecting, preserving, guiding, and leading them to clearer light and higher life. The attribute *ar-Raḥmān* (Most Gracious) is not applied to anyone but God, but the attribute *Raḥīm* (Merciful) is a general term and may be applied to humans as well.

To remind us of these boundless gifts of God is the formula: "In the Name of God, Most Gracious, Most Merciful" which is found at the beginning of every *Sūrah* of the Qur'ān (except the ninth), and is repeated by a Muslim at the beginning of almost every act he undertakes.

2: The Arabic word *Rabb*, usually translated as 'Lord', also carries the meaning of creating, supporting, sustaining, and bringing to maturity. In His kindness, God, cares for all the worlds He has created.

3: {The two names of God, *ar-Raḥmān* and *ar-Raḥīm,* are once again repeated here, emphasizing how important the Divine attributes of Mercy are for us. AG}

4: {On the Day of Judgement, Allāh ﷻ will be the sole Master and Owner. All will be totally dependent on His Mercy and Justice. In this life, He has given us limited freedom to act and limited ownership of possessions for a limited period of time. AG}

5: Once we recognize God's Love, Mercy, Power and Justice (as Ruler of the Day of Judgement), we must submit to Him completely. We worship Him alone and ask for His aid only, for there is none other worthy of our worship, and none other that will help us.

6: "Guide us to and in the straight Way." Spiritually, we may be wandering aimlessly. Thus, the first step is to find the Way. The second step is to remain steadfast in the Way. When our own wisdom may fail, we must ask for Allāh's Guidance. With a little spiritual insight, we shall see those who walk in the light of God's Grace, and those who walk in the darkness of His Wrath. {The Qur'ān, "the Book that is guidance to the righteous," (*Al-Baqarah* 2:2) is sent as an answer to this prayer of guidance. The *Sunnah* of Rasūlullāh ﷺ teaches how to walk steadily on that Way. AG}

7: The Wrath (*al-Ghaḍab*) is the opposite of the Grace, Peace and Harmony (*al-In`ām*). Note that our own actions are responsible for losing His Grace and inviting His Wrath. Apparently, there are two kinds of people deserving of this Wrath (*al-Maghḍūb*): those who choose to be in the darkness of Wrath through their evil actions, and those who carelessly go astray. The first are those who deliberately break God's Law; the second are those who go astray out of carelessness. Both are responsible for their own acts or omissions. {The first kind does not receive guidance and their hearts are sealed from receiving any Light (*Al-Baqarah* 2:6-7). The second kind is given the chance to return to the Straight Path, if they sincerely repent. For such people, the Qur'ān and the *Sunnah* of Rasūlullāh ﷺ awaits to guide them and Allāh's Grace will forgive and accept them. AG}
On the other hand, there are the righteous people, who have chosen to be in the light of God's Mercy. His Mercy not only protects them from wrongdoing (as they have already submitted their will to Him), but it also continuously guides them to the Way of the blessed (see 4:69).

IMPORTANT POINTS TO LEARN AND REFLECT UPON

- Allāh ﷻ is Most Gracious and Most Merciful.
- We should worship Him alone and ask only His help in all matters.
- The best prayer that we should make to Him is to give us guidance and to keep us on the Straight Path.

GLOSSARY WORDS

Al-Fātiḥah, Rabb al-`Ālamīn, Umm al-Kitāb, Al-Ghaḍab, Al-Maghḍūb, Grace

VOCABULARY

١-سورة الفاتحة

(١) بِسْمِ ٱللّٰهِ	In the Name of Allah
اَلرَّحْمٰنِ	The Most Gracious, The Beneficent
اَلرَّحِيْمِ	the Most Merciful
(٢) اَلْ	The (definite article)
حَمْدُ	praise
لِلّٰهِ	for, due to
رَبِّ	Lord, Allah
اَلْعَالَمِيْنَ	(of) the worlds
(٣) اَلرَّحْمٰنِ	The Most Merciful
اَلرَّحِيْمِ	The Most Kind
(٤) مٰلِكِ	Master, Owner
يومِ	Day (of)
اَلدِّيْنِ	The Judgement
(٥) إِيَّاكَ	(to) You alone, only to You
نَعْبُدُ	We worship
وَ	and
إِيَّاكَ	(from) You alone
نَسْتَعِيْنُ	we seek aid, help
(٦) إِهْدِنَا	Show us, guide us
اَلصِّرَاطَ	the way, the path
اَلْمُسْتَقِيْمَ	the straight, smooth
(٧) صِرَاطَ	way, path (of)
اَلَّذِيْنَ	those, who
أَنْعَمْتَ	You favored
عَلَىٰ	on, upon
هِمْ	them
غَيْرِ	not of those
اَلْمَغْضُوبِ	who earned the anger
عَلَيْهِمْ	on them
وَ	and
لاَ	not, neither
اَلضَّآلِّيْنَ	who went astray, went off the path

Section 1: 1-12

سُورَةُ يسٓ

SŪRAH YĀ-SĪN 36: 1-83

Yā Sīn / Yā Sīn

Name: The *Sūrah* takes its name from the two separated letters *(Ḥurūf al-Muqaṭṭa`āt) Yā* and *Sīn.* We do not know their exact meaning, but in popular tradition, it is considered to be a title of Rasūlullāh ﷺ.

Period of Revelation: The style of this *Sūrah* indicates that it belongs to the middle Makkan period.

Subject Matter and Theme: Rasūlullāh ﷺ said, "For everything there is a heart (*al-Qalb*), and the heart of the Qur'ān is *Sūrah Yā Sīn.* I want that every one of my *'Ummah* takes it to the heart."

The object of this *Sūrah* is to teach the central Islamic doctrines concerning:

1. the *Tawḥīd*
2. the *Ākhirah* (the Hereafter)
3. the Truth of the Revelation and of the Prophethood of Rasūlullāh ﷺ.

It is related by Ma'qil bin Yasar ﷺ that Rasūlullāh ﷺ said: "Recite *Sūrah Yā Sīn* to the dying ones among you." The purpose of this is to refresh Islamic teachings and thoughts of the Hereafter in the mind of the dying person.

ARABIC TEXT

بِسْمِ ٱللَّهِ ٱلرَّحْمَٰنِ ٱلرَّحِيمِ

يسٓ ﴿١﴾ وَٱلْقُرْءَانِ ٱلْحَكِيمِ ﴿٢﴾ إِنَّكَ لَمِنَ ٱلْمُرْسَلِينَ ﴿٣﴾ عَلَىٰ

صِرَٰطٍ مُّسْتَقِيمٍ ﴿٤﴾ تَنزِيلَ ٱلْعَزِيزِ ٱلرَّحِيمِ ﴿٥﴾ لِتُنذِرَ قَوْمًا مَّآ

أُنذِرَ ءَابَآؤُهُمْ فَهُمْ غَٰفِلُونَ ﴿٦﴾ لَقَدْ حَقَّ ٱلْقَوْلُ عَلَىٰٓ أَكْثَرِهِمْ

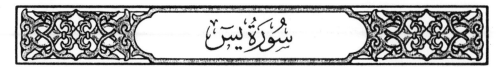

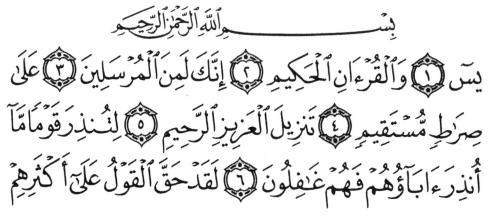

فَهُمْ لَا يُؤْمِنُونَ ﴿٧﴾ إِنَّا جَعَلْنَا فِىٓ أَعْنَٰقِهِمْ أَغْلَٰلًا فَهِىَ إِلَى
ٱلْأَذْقَانِ فَهُم مُّقْمَحُونَ ﴿٨﴾ وَجَعَلْنَا مِنۢ بَيْنِ أَيْدِيهِمْ سَدًّا
وَمِنْ خَلْفِهِمْ سَدًّا فَأَغْشَيْنَٰهُمْ فَهُمْ لَا يُبْصِرُونَ ﴿٩﴾ وَسَوَآءٌ
عَلَيْهِمْ ءَأَنذَرْتَهُمْ أَمْ لَمْ تُنذِرْهُمْ لَا يُؤْمِنُونَ ﴿١٠﴾ إِنَّمَا تُنذِرُ
مَنِ ٱتَّبَعَ ٱلذِّكْرَ وَخَشِىَ ٱلرَّحْمَٰنَ بِٱلْغَيْبِ ۖ فَبَشِّرْهُ بِمَغْفِرَةٍ
وَأَجْرٍ كَرِيمٍ ﴿١١﴾ إِنَّا نَحْنُ نُحْىِ ٱلْمَوْتَىٰ وَنَكْتُبُ
مَا قَدَّمُوا۟ وَءَاثَٰرَهُمْ ۚ وَكُلَّ شَىْءٍ أَحْصَيْنَٰهُ فِىٓ إِمَامٍ مُّبِينٍ ﴿١٢﴾

TRANSLATIONS

1. Yā Sīn.
2. By the Qur'ān, full of Wisdom -
3. You are indeed one of the messengers,
4. On a Straight Way.
5. It is a Revelation sent down by (Him), the Exalted in Might, Most Merciful,
6. In order that you may admonish a people, whose fathers had received no admonition, and who therefore remain heedless (of the Signs of Allāh).
7. The Word is proved true against the greater part of them; for they do not believe.
8. We have put yokes round their necks right up to their chins, so that their heads

1. Yā Sīn.
2. By the wise Qur'ān,
3. Lo! you are of those sent
4. On a straight path,
5. A revelation of the Mighty, the Merciful,
6. That you may warn a folk whose fathers were not warned, so they are heedless.
7. Already has the word proved true of most of them, for they believe not.
8. Lo! we have put on their necks carcans reaching unto the chins, so that they are

are forced up (and they cannot see).

9. And We have put a bar in front of them and a bar behind them, and further, We have covered them up; so that they cannot see.

10. The same is it to them whether you admonish them or you do not admonish them: they will not believe.

11. You can but admonish: such a one as follows the Message and fears the (Lord) Most Gracious, unseen: give such a one, therefore, good tidings, of Forgiveness and a Reward most generous.

12. Verily We shall give life to the dead, and We record that which they sent before and that which they leave behind, and of all things have We taken account in a clear Book (of evidence).

(A. Y. Ali)

made stiff necked.

9. And We have set a bar before them and a bar behind them, and (thus) have covered them so that they see not.

10. Whether you warn them or you warn them not, it is alike for them, for they believe not.

11. You warn only him who follows the Reminder and fears the Beneficent in secret. To him bear tidings of forgiveness and a rich reward.

12. Lo! We it is Who bring the dead to life. We record that which they send before (them), and their footprints. And all things We have kept in a clear register.

(M. M. Pickthal)

EXPLANATION (A. Y. Ali, revised)

1: *Yā-Sīn* is usually treated as a title of the Holy Prophet ﷺ. No final assertion can be made about *Yā Sīn*, the two *Ḥurūf al-Muqaṭṭa`āt* (the Abbreviated Letters).
Some commentators take *Yā* meaning "O" and *Sīn* to be the abbreviation of *Insān* (humankind). Thus, it would be an address to humans: "O Humans!" "Human" in this connection refers to the Leader of humans, the noblest of Humankind, Muḥammad ﷺ, as this *Sūrah* mainly deals with the Holy Prophet ﷺ and his message.

2-3: The best qualities of the Holy Prophet ﷺ are:

(1) the undoubted Revelation he brought (the Qur'ān)

(2) the unselfish and perfect life he led (on a Straight Way)

The appeal is, therefore, made on the testimony of these two facts.

4-5: The Revelation again is characterized by two attributes which we find most helpful in being mindful of Allāh ﷻ:

(1) It has force and power, for Allāh ﷻ is Exalted in Might and able to enforce His Will effortlessly.

(2) It brings a message of hope and mercy, for Allāh ﷻ is Most Merciful.

By these characteristics, we know that the guidance of the Qur'ān is from Allāh ﷻ.

6: The Quraish had never before received a Prophet. Thus, one of their own was made the Last Messenger, to deliver the final and universal Message for all mankind.

7: If people deliberately refuse "to believe," i.e., to receive guidance, Allāh's Grace and Mercy are withdrawn from them. Their own disobedience blocks all channels for their correction.

8-9: Human misdeeds lead to the enforcement of Allāh's Law. The result of human disobedience is described in a series of metaphors:

(1) Rejection of Allāh's Light results in the yoke of sin being tied around the human neck. It tightens steadily as disobedience becomes more severe.

(2) The head is forced up and kept in a stiff position. Disobedience is not only grave error in itself; it also leads to greater sins.

(3) This state of deprivation of Allāh's Mercy leads to such a decline in spiritual power that the sinner can neither progress nor turn back.

(4) His return is cut off, and his progression becomes impossible. Furthermore, the Light that comes from Heaven is cut off, so that he loses all hope.

10: When such a stage of utter hopelessness is reached, revelation or spiritual teaching ceases to hold any value for them. {Preaching is still our responsibility; only Allāh ﷻ will decide who is righteous, and who is to be deprived of His Message. AG}.

11: However, there are others who, while not yet fully aware of the Truth, are ready to hear Allāh's Message and receive His Guidance. They love Allāh ﷻ and fear violating His Holy Law. While they do not see Allāh ﷻ, they feel His presence as if they are seeing Him. To such persons, the Message of Allāh ﷻ comes as good news; it promises them forgiveness for any past wrongdoing, and it gives them hope of a full reward in the future.

12: All this is possible because there is the assurance of a Hereafter in which Allāh ﷻ will be the final Judge. Our deeds, good and bad, will be brought to our account. Our account will also continue to grow by those actions, good and bad, that continue after our earthly life has ceased.

Our moral and spiritual responsibility is, therefore, much greater than just as it affects us today. {We must sincerely work for the Hereafter and leave behind *Ṣadaqah al-Jāriyah*, "Continuing charity," to increase our share of the rewards of the Hereafter. AG}

IMPORTANT POINTS TO LEARN AND REFLECT UPON

- The Qur'ān is the Divine revelation sent by the Merciful Lord to His final, chosen Messenger.
- Those who do not accept the revelation out of pride, even after its truth has been established, are deprived of all guidance.
- The Qur'ān is good news for those who willingly follow the message and love and fear Allāh ﷻ.

GLOSSARY WORDS

Tawḥīd, Ṣadaqah al-Jāriyah

VOCABULARY

سورة يس - ٣٦

الركوع ١ - Section 1

بِسْمِ ٱللَّهِ ٱلرَّحْمَٰنِ ٱلرَّحِيمِ

(١) يٰسٓ	Yasin, O human	(٤) عَلَىٰ صِرَٰطٍ	On a Way
(٢) وَٱلْقُرْءَانِ	By the Qur'an	مُّسْتَقِيمٍ	straight
ٱلْحَكِيمِ	full of wisdom	(٥) تَنزِيلَ	It is a revelation sent down
(٣) إِنَّكَ	You are indeed	ٱلْعَزِيزِ	The Exalted in Might
لَمِنَ ٱلْمُرْسَلِينَ	one of the messengers	ٱلرَّحِيمِ	the Most Merciful

(٦) لِتُنذِرَ	You may warn	وَمِنْ خَلْفِهِمْ	And behind them
قَوْمًا	a people	سَدًّا	a bar
مَّآ أُنذِرَ	that were not warned	فَأَغْشَيْنَٰهُمْ	so, We have covered them up
ءَابَآؤُهُمْ	their fathers	فَهُمْ لَا يُبْصِرُونَ	so that they cannot see
فَهُمْ	and who therefore	(١٠) وَسَوَآءٌ عَلَيْهِمْ	The same is it to them
غَٰفِلُونَ	remain heedless	ءَأَنذَرْتَهُمْ	whether you admonish them
(٧) لَقَدْ حَقَّ ٱلْقَوْلُ	The word is proved true	أَمْ لَمْ تُنذِرْهُمْ	or you do not admonish them
عَلَىٰٓ أَكْثَرِهِمْ	Against the greater part of them	لَا يُؤْمِنُونَ	they will not believe
فَهُمْ لَا يُؤْمِنُونَ	for they do not believe	(١١) إِنَّمَا تُنذِرُ	You can only admonish
(٨) إِنَّا جَعَلْنَا	We have put	مَنِ ٱتَّبَعَ	such a one as follows
فِىٓ أَعْنَٰقِهِمْ	round their necks	ٱلذِّكْرَ	the Message
فَهِيَ إِلَى ٱلْأَذْقَانِ	it is right up to their chins	وَخَشِيَ	and fears
أَغْلَٰلًا	yokes	ٱلرَّحْمَٰنَ	the Most Gracious
فَهُم	so that their	بِٱلْغَيْبِ	unseen
مُّقْمَحُونَ	heads are forced up	فَبَشِّرْهُ	give such a one good tidings
(٩) وَجَعَلْنَا	And We have put	بِمَغْفِرَةٍ	of forgiveness
مِنۢ بَيْنِ أَيْدِيهِمْ	in front of them	وَأَجْرٍ	and a reward
سَدًّا	a bar	كَرِيمٍ	most generous

(١٢) إِنَّا نَحْنُ	Verily We	وَءَاثَـٰرَهُمْ	and that which they leave behind
نُحْيِ	shall give life	وَكُلَّ شَىْءٍ	and of all things
الْمَوْتَىٰ	to the dead	أَحْصَيْنَـٰهُ	have We taken account
وَنَكْتُبُ	and We record	فِي إِمَامٍ	in a book (of evidence)
مَا قَدَّمُوا	that which they send before	مُّبِينٍ	clear

Section 2: 13-32

SŪRAH YĀ-SĪN 36

Yā Sīn / Yā Sīn

ARABIC TEXT

بِسْمِ اللَّهِ الرَّحْمَـٰنِ الرَّحِيمِ

وَاضْرِبْ لَهُم مَّثَلًا أَصْحَـٰبَ الْقَرْيَةِ إِذْ جَاءَهَا الْمُرْسَلُونَ ﴿١٣﴾
إِذْ أَرْسَلْنَا إِلَيْهِمُ اثْنَيْنِ فَكَذَّبُوهُمَا فَعَزَّزْنَا بِثَالِثٍ فَقَالُوا إِنَّا
إِلَيْكُم مُّرْسَلُونَ ﴿١٤﴾ قَالُوا مَا أَنتُمْ إِلَّا بَشَرٌ مِّثْلُنَا وَمَا أَنزَلَ
الرَّحْمَـٰنُ مِن شَيْءٍ إِنْ أَنتُمْ إِلَّا تَكْذِبُونَ ﴿١٥﴾ قَالُوا رَبُّنَا يَعْلَمُ إِنَّا
إِلَيْكُمْ لَمُرْسَلُونَ ﴿١٦﴾ وَمَا عَلَيْنَا إِلَّا الْبَلَـٰغُ الْمُبِينُ ﴿١٧﴾
قَالُوا إِنَّا تَطَيَّرْنَا بِكُمْ لَئِن لَّمْ تَنتَهُوا لَنَرْجُمَنَّكُمْ وَلَيَمَسَّنَّكُم
مِّنَّا عَذَابٌ أَلِيمٌ ﴿١٨﴾ قَالُوا طَـٰئِرُكُم مَّعَكُمْ أَئِن ذُكِّرْتُم
بَلْ أَنتُمْ قَوْمٌ مُّسْرِفُونَ ﴿١٩﴾ وَجَاءَ مِنْ أَقْصَا الْمَدِينَةِ رَجُلٌ
يَسْعَىٰ قَالَ يَـٰقَوْمِ اتَّبِعُوا الْمُرْسَلِينَ ﴿٢٠﴾ اتَّبِعُوا مَن
لَّا يَسْأَلُكُمْ أَجْرًا وَهُم مُّهْتَدُونَ ﴿٢١﴾ وَمَا لِيَ لَا أَعْبُدُ الَّذِي
فَطَرَنِي وَإِلَيْهِ تُرْجَعُونَ ﴿٢٢﴾ ءَأَتَّخِذُ مِن دُونِهِۦ ءَالِهَةً إِن
يُرِدْنِ الرَّحْمَـٰنُ بِضُرٍّ لَّا تُغْنِ عَنِّي شَفَـٰعَتُهُمْ شَيْئًا وَلَا

يُنقِذُونِ ﴿٢٣﴾ إِنِّيٓ إِذٗا لَّفِي ضَلَٰلٖ مُّبِينٍ ﴿٢٤﴾ إِنِّيٓ ءَامَنتُ
بِرَبِّكُمۡ فَٱسۡمَعُونِ ﴿٢٥﴾ قِيلَ ٱدۡخُلِ ٱلۡجَنَّةَۖ قَالَ يَٰلَيۡتَ قَوۡمِي
يَعۡلَمُونَ ﴿٢٦﴾ بِمَا غَفَرَ لِي رَبِّي وَجَعَلَنِي مِنَ ٱلۡمُكۡرَمِينَ ﴿٢٧﴾
۞وَمَآ أَنزَلۡنَا عَلَىٰ قَوۡمِهِۦ مِنۢ بَعۡدِهِۦ مِن جُندٖ مِّنَ ٱلسَّمَآءِ وَمَا
كُنَّا مُنزِلِينَ ﴿٢٨﴾ إِن كَانَتۡ إِلَّا صَيۡحَةٗ وَٰحِدَةٗ فَإِذَا هُمۡ خَٰمِدُونَ
﴿٢٩﴾ يَٰحَسۡرَةً عَلَى ٱلۡعِبَادِۚ مَا يَأۡتِيهِم مِّن رَّسُولٍ إِلَّا كَانُواْ بِهِۦ
يَسۡتَهۡزِءُونَ ﴿٣٠﴾ أَلَمۡ يَرَوۡاْ كَمۡ أَهۡلَكۡنَا قَبۡلَهُم مِّنَ ٱلۡقُرُونِ
أَنَّهُمۡ إِلَيۡهِمۡ لَا يَرۡجِعُونَ ﴿٣١﴾ وَإِن كُلّٞ لَّمَّا جَمِيعٞ لَّدَيۡنَا مُحۡضَرُونَ ﴿٣٢﴾

TRANSLATIONS

13. Set forth to them, by way of a parable {*Mat͟halan*}, the (story of) the Companions of the City. Behold, there came messengers to it.

14. When We (first) sent to them two messengers, they rejected them: but We strengthened them with a third: they said, "Truly, we have been sent on a mission to you."

15. The (people) said: "You are only men like ourselves; and (Allāh) Most Gracious sends no sort of revelation: You do

13. Coin for them a similitude: The people of the city when those sent (from Allāh) came unto them;

14. When We sent unto them twain, and they denied them both, so We reinforced them with a third, and they said: Lo! we have been sent unto you.

15. They said: You are but mortals like unto us. The Beneficent has naught revealed. You do but lie!

nothing but lie."

16. They said: "Our Lord does know that we have been sent on a mission to you:

17. "And Our duty is only to proclaim *{Al-Balāgh}* the clear Message."

18. The (people) said "For us, we augur an evil omen *{taṭṭayarah}* from you: if you desist not, we will certainly stone you, and a grievous punishment indeed will be inflicted on you by us."

19. They said: "Your evil omens are with ourselves: (deem you this an evil omen), if you are admonished? Nay, but you are a people transgressing all bounds!"

20. Then there came running, from the farthest part of the City, a person, saying, "O my people! obey the messengers:

21. "Obey those who ask no reward of you (for themselves), and who have themselves received Guidance.

22. "It would not be reasonable in me if I did not serve Him Who created me, and to Whom you shall (all) be brought back.

23. "Shall I take (other) gods *{āliha}* besides Him? If (Allāh) Most Gracious should intend some adversity for me, of no use whatever will be their intercession for me, nor can they deliver me.

24. "I would indeed, if I were to do so, be in manifest Error.

25. "For me, I have faith in the Lord of you (all): listen, then, to me!"

26. It was said: "Enter you the Garden *{Jannah}*." He said "Ah me! would that

16. They answered: Our Lord knows that we are indeed sent unto you,

17. And our duty is but plain conveyance (of the message).

18. (The people of the city) said: We augur ill of you. If you desist not, we shall surely stone you, and grievous torture will befall you at our hands.

19. They said: Your evil augury be with you! Is it because you are reminded (of the truth)? Nay, but you are froward folk?

20. And there came from the uttermost part of the city a man running. He cried: O my people! Follow those who have been sent!

21. Follow those who ask of you no fee, and who are rightly guided.

22. For what cause should I not serve Him Who has created me, and unto Whom you will be brought back?

23. Shall I take (other) gods in place of Him when, if the Beneficent should wish me any harm, their intercession will avail me naught, nor can they save?

24. Then truly I should be in error manifest.

25. Lo! I have believed in your Lord, so hear me!

26. It was said (unto him): Enter Paradise. He said: Would that my people knew

my People knew (what I know)!-

27. "For that my Lord has granted me Forgiveness and has enrolled me among those held in honor!"

28. And We sent not down against his People, after Him, any hosts from heaven, nor was it needful for Us so to do.

29. It was no more than a single mighty Blast, and behold! they were (like ashes) quenched and silent.

30. Ah! alas for (My) servants! There comes not a messenger {*Rasūl*} to them but they mock him!

31. See they not how many generations before them We destroyed? Not to them will they return:

32. But each one of them all - will be brought before Us (for judgement).

(A. Y. Ali)

27. With what (munificence) my Lord has pardoned me and made me of the honored ones!

28. We sent not down against his people after him a host from heaven, nor do We ever send.

29. It was but one Shout, and lo! they were extinct.

30. Ah, the anguish for the bondmen! Never came there unto them a messenger but they did mock him!

31. Have they not seen how many generations We destroyed before them, which indeed return not unto them;

32. But all, without exception, will be brought before Us?

(M. M. Pickthal)

EXPLANATION (M. Y. Ali, revised)

13: Many of the classical commentators believe that the City referred to here was Antioch, one of the most important cities in North Syria during the first century of the Christian era. Following Ibn Kat͟hīr, the famous commentator, I reject the identification with Antioch decisively. No name, period, or place is mentioned in the text. The significance of the story is in the lessons to be derived from it as a parable that is independent of name, time, or place.

14: Allāh ﷻ sent His messengers alone or in pairs, to areas where opposition to the Truth was great and where He considered it necessary. He supported them with others that followed. Their Mission was Divine, but they did not claim to be more than common human beings. This was used by the unjust and the ungodly as a disqualification.

Their Universal Message exposed the evil ways of society and selfish people thought it unlucky. It was often seen that when a messenger came, the poorest and most despised among the ranks (from "farthest parts of the City") were the ones who accepted the Message and were willing to work, live and die for it.

15: The unjust not only rejected the mission of their particular messengers, they also denied the possibility of Allāh ﷻ sending such missions through ordinary human beings.

16: Just as an ordinary messenger, whose credentials are doubted, can refer to the authority granted by his superior as ultimate proof of his mission, so these messengers of Allāh ﷻ invoked His authority as of the truth of their mission.

17: Then, they proceeded to explain what their mission was. It was not to force them, but rather to convince them. It was to proclaim Allāh's Laws which the people were defying openly and clearly.

18: *Aṭ-Ṭair,* means 'the bird.' The Arabs superstitiously derived omens from birds. From *Ṭair* (bird) came *ta-ṭaiyara,* or *ṭṭaiyara,* to draw evil omens. Because the prophets of Allāh ﷻ denounced evil, the evil-doers believed that they brought bad luck to them.

19: "What you call bad omens arises from your own misdeeds. Do you suppose that a man who comes to warn you and teach you a better way brings you ill-luck?" This is the very height of disobedience!

20: While the wealthy and influential people in the city were doubtful of Allāh's plans, the truth was seen by a man from the outskirts; the poor section of the City; held in low esteem by the rich. This righteous person believed, and he wished his fellow countrymen also to believe.
Similarly, when the arrogant chiefs of the Quraish exiled the Prophet ﷺ, it was the people of Madīnah, the *Anṣār* (from the outskirts), who welcomed him, believed in him, and supported his mission.

21: The Prophets and their true followers do not seek to heighten their own advantage. They serve Allāh ﷻ and humanity. Their hope lies in the good pleasure of Allāh ﷻ, in Whose service they remain devoted.

22: The argument throughout is that of a strong personal conviction of the individual himself. It is combined with an appeal to his people to follow the Straight Path and experience the benefit of the spiritual satisfaction which he himself has achieved.

23: The next plea is to submit exclusively to Allāh ﷻ. All power belongs to Him. If, in His Universal Plan, He may think fit to test me with some sorrow or punish me for my fault, would these imaginary and false deities help me or intercede on my behalf? Not at all.

25: If, in fact, I trust these idols and deities, I would blatantly go astray and wander away from the True Path.

25: Again, one sees the transition from a personal conviction to an appeal to everyone to benefit from the speaker's experience. "I have found the fullest satisfaction for my soul in Allāh ﷻ. Will you not follow my advice, and prove for yourselves that the Lord is indeed Merciful?"

26: This godly and righteous man entered into the Garden (*Jannah*). Perhaps, it is implied that he was blessed with martyrdom. But even then, his thoughts were always with the guidance of his people. He regretted their disobedience and wished even then that they might repent and obtain salvation.

27: This man was just a simple honest soul, but he heard and obeyed the call of the prophets and obtained spiritual contentment for himself and did his best to bring salvation to his people. All his past was forgiven, and he was raised in dignity and honor in the Kingdom of Heaven.

28-29: Allāh's Punishment does not necessarily come with announcement and warning. A single mighty blast, either the rumbling of an earthquake or a great and violent wind, was sufficient in this case. (See also note from *Hūd* 11:67 which describes the fate of the Thamūd; also *An-'Ankabūt* 29:40 note).

30: Ignorant people laugh at Allāh's prophets and ultimately ruin their own lives. If they study history, they will see that countless generations were destroyed before them, because they did not take the truth seriously. The term "servants" here is equivalent to 'people.' Allāh ﷻ regrets the folly of humans, especially as He cherishes us as His own creatures.

31-32: The earlier generations that We have destroyed before the people addressed ('do they not see?') will not be restored. They enjoyed prosperity and good fortune, but they were wiped out because of their disobedience. They will not be restored in this life, but all people will be brought before Us on the Day of Judgement to give an account of their past deeds.

IMPORTANT POINTS TO LEARN AND REFLECT UPON

- Whenever a messenger or the righteous followers came with the Message, the leaders of the community rejected them out of their own selfishness.
- Allāh's Cause is often supported by common people.
- Allāh ﷻ does not punish anyone without first giving him/her the opportunity to accept the truth and follow the right path.

GLOSSARY WORDS

al-Balāgh, *āliha,* conviction, credential, *mathalan*, omen, parable, *taṭṭayyara*

VOCABULARY

الركوع ٢ - Section 2

بِسْمِ ٱللَّهِ ٱلرَّحْمَٰنِ ٱلرَّحِيمِ

(١٣) وَٱضْرِبْ لَهُم	Set forth to them	ٱثْنَيْنِ	two (messengers)
مَّثَلًا	by way of a parable	فَكَذَّبُوهُمَا	so they rejected them
أَصْحَٰبَ	the Companions (of)	فَعَزَّزْنَا	but We strengthened them
ٱلْقَرْيَةِ	the City	بِثَالِثٍ	with a third
إِذْ جَآءَهَا	at the time came to it	فَقَالُوٓا	so they said
ٱلْمُرْسَلُونَ	the messengers	إِنَّآ	truly, we
(١٤) إِذْ أَرْسَلْنَآ	When We sent	إِلَيْكُم	to you
إِلَيْهِمُ	to them	مُّرْسَلُونَ	have been sent

(١٥) قَالُوا	The (people) said	مِنَّا عَذَابٌ	by us a punishment
مَآ أَنتُمْ إِلاَّ بَشَرٌ	you are only human	أَلِيمٌ	grievous
مِّثْلُنَا	like ourselves	١٩-قَالُوا	They said
وَمَآ أَنزَلَ	and sends not	طَـٰئِرُكُم	your evil omens
ٱلرَّحْمَـٰنُ	the Most Gracious	مَّعَكُمْ	are with yourselves
مِن شَىْءٍ	any thing (of revelation)	أَئِن ذُكِّرْتُم	If you are admonished
إِنْ أَنتُم	you rather (do nothing)	بَلْ أَنْتُمْ قَوْمٌ	but you are a people
إِلاَّ تَكْذِبُونَ	but lie	مُّسْرِفُونَ	transgressing all bounds
١٦-قَالُوا	they said	٢٠-وَجَآءَ	Then there came
رَبُّنَا	our Lord	مِنْ أَقْصَا	from the farthest part
يَعْلَمُ	knows	ٱلْمَدِينَةِ	of the city
إِنَّا إِلَيْكُمْ	we have been sent to you	رَجُلٌ	a man
لَمُرْسَلُونَ	on a mission	يَسْعَىٰ قَالَ	running, saying
١٧-وَمَا عَلَيْنَآ إِلاَّ	And our duty is only	يَـٰقَوْمِ	O my people
ٱلْبَلَـٰغُ ٱلْمُبِينُ	to proclaim the clear Message	ٱتَّبِعُوا	obey
١٨-قَالُوٓا	The (people) said	ٱلْمُرْسَلِينَ	the messengers
إِنَّا تَطَيَّرْنَا	we augur an evil omen	(٢١) ٱتَّبِعُوا	Obey
بِكُمْ	from you	مَن لاَّ يَسْـَٔلُكُمْ	those who ask nothing of you
لَئِن لَّمْ تَنتَهُوا	if you desist not	أَجْرًا	of reward
لَنَرْجُمَنَّكُمْ	we will certainly stone you	وَهُم	and who
وَلَيَمَسَّنَّكُم	and will be inflicted	مُّهْتَدُونَ	have received guidance

(٢٢) وَمَالِىَ	Why should I	(٢٦) قِيلَ	It was said
لاَ أَعْبُدُ	not serve, not worship	أُدْخُلِ الْجَنَّةَ	Enter you the Garden
الَّذِى فَطَرَنِى	Him who created me	قَالَ يٰلَيْتَ	Ah me! Would that
وَ إِلَيْهِ	and to Whom	قَوْمِى	my people
تُرْجَعُونَ	you shall be brought back	يَعْلَمُونَ	knew (what I know)
(٢٣) ءَأَتَّخِذُ	Shall I take other	(٢٧) بِمَا غَفَرَلِى	For that granted me forgiveness
مِنْ دُونِهِ	than Him (besides Him)	رَبِّى	my Lord
اٰلِهَةً	(as) Gods	وَجَعَلَنِى	and has enrolled me
إِنْ يُرِدْنِ	if intends for me	مِنَ الْمُكْرَمِينَ	among those held in honor
الرَّحْمٰنُ	Most Gracious	(٢٨) وَمَآ أَنْزَلْنَا	And We sent not down
بِضُرٍّ	some adversity	عَلٰى قَوْمِهِ	against his people
لاَّ تُغْنِ عَنِّى	of no use for me	مِنْ بَعْدِهِ	after him
شَفَاعَتُهُمْ	their intercession	مِنْ جُنْدٍ	any hosts
شَيْئًا	at all	مِّنَ السَّمَآءِ	from heaven
وَّ لاَ يُنْقِذُونِ	nor can they deliver me	وَمَا كُنَّا مُنْزِلِينَ	nor was it needful for Us so to do
(٢٤) إِنِّىٓ	I would indeed	(٢٩) إِنْ كَانَتْ إِلاَّ	It was no more than
إِذًا لَّفِى	If I were to do so be	صَيْحَةً وَّاحِدَةً	a single mighty blast
ضَلٰلٍ مُّبِينٍ	in manifest error	فَإِذَا هُمْ خٰمِدُونَ	behold! they were (like ashes)
(٢٥) إِنِّىٓ اٰمَنْتُ	For me, I have faith	(٣٠) يٰحَسْرَةً	Ah! alas
بِرَبِّكُمْ	in the Lord of you (all)	عَلَى الْعِبَادِ	for (the) servants
فَاسْمَعُونِ	listen, then, to me	مَا يَأْتِيهِمْ	There comes not to them

مَنْ رَسُولٍ	a messenger	أَنَّهُمْ إِلَيْهِمْ	not to them
إِلاَّ كَانُوا بِهِ	but they to him	لاَ يَرْجِعُونَ	will they return
يَسْتَهْزِءُونَ	they mock (him)	(٣٢) وَ إِنْ كُلٌّ	But each one of them
(٣١) أَلَمْ يَرَوا	See they not	لَمَّا جَمِيعٌ	all without exception
كَمْ أَهْلَكْنَا	how many We destroyed	لَدَيْنَا	before Us (for judgment)
قَبْلَهُمْ مِنَ الْقُرُونِ	before them, of generation	مُحْضَرُونَ	will be brought

Section 3: 33-50

SŪRAH YĀ-SĪN 36

Yā Sīn / Yā Sīn

ARABIC TEXT

بِسْمِ ٱللَّهِ ٱلرَّحْمَٰنِ ٱلرَّحِيمِ

وَءَايَةٌ لَّهُمُ ٱلْأَرْضُ ٱلْمَيْتَةُ أَحْيَيْنَٰهَا وَأَخْرَجْنَا مِنْهَا حَبًّا
فَمِنْهُ يَأْكُلُونَ ٣٣ وَجَعَلْنَا فِيهَا جَنَّٰتٍ مِّن نَّخِيلٍ
وَأَعْنَٰبٍ وَفَجَّرْنَا فِيهَا مِنَ ٱلْعُيُونِ ٣٤ لِيَأْكُلُوا۟ مِن ثَمَرِهِۦ
وَمَا عَمِلَتْهُ أَيْدِيهِمْ ۖ أَفَلَا يَشْكُرُونَ ٣٥ سُبْحَٰنَ ٱلَّذِى
خَلَقَ ٱلْأَزْوَٰجَ كُلَّهَا مِمَّا تُنۢبِتُ ٱلْأَرْضُ وَمِنْ أَنفُسِهِمْ
وَمِمَّا لَا يَعْلَمُونَ ٣٦ وَءَايَةٌ لَّهُمُ ٱلَّيْلُ نَسْلَخُ مِنْهُ ٱلنَّهَارَ
فَإِذَا هُم مُّظْلِمُونَ ٣٧ وَٱلشَّمْسُ تَجْرِى لِمُسْتَقَرٍّ لَّهَا ۚ
ذَٰلِكَ تَقْدِيرُ ٱلْعَزِيزِ ٱلْعَلِيمِ ٣٨ وَٱلْقَمَرَ قَدَّرْنَٰهُ مَنَازِلَ حَتَّىٰ
عَادَ كَٱلْعُرْجُونِ ٱلْقَدِيمِ ٣٩ لَا ٱلشَّمْسُ يَنۢبَغِى لَهَآ أَن تُدْرِكَ
ٱلْقَمَرَ وَلَا ٱلَّيْلُ سَابِقُ ٱلنَّهَارِ ۚ وَكُلٌّ فِى فَلَكٍ يَسْبَحُونَ ٤٠
وَءَايَةٌ لَّهُمْ أَنَّا حَمَلْنَا ذُرِّيَّتَهُمْ فِى ٱلْفُلْكِ ٱلْمَشْحُونِ ٤١ وَخَلَقْنَا
لَهُم مِّن مِّثْلِهِۦ مَا يَرْكَبُونَ ٤٢ وَإِن نَّشَأْ نُغْرِقْهُمْ فَلَا صَرِيخَ لَهُمْ
وَلَا هُمْ يُنقَذُونَ ٤٣ إِلَّا رَحْمَةً مِّنَّا وَمَتَٰعًا إِلَىٰ حِينٍ ٤٤ وَإِذَا

قِيلَ لَهُمُ ٱتَّقُوا۟ مَا بَيْنَ أَيْدِيكُمْ وَمَا خَلْفَكُمْ لَعَلَّكُمْ تُرْحَمُونَ ﴿٤٥﴾
وَمَا تَأْتِيهِم مِّنْ ءَايَةٍ مِّنْ ءَايَٰتِ رَبِّهِمْ إِلَّا كَانُوا۟ عَنْهَا مُعْرِضِينَ
﴿٤٦﴾ وَإِذَا قِيلَ لَهُمْ أَنفِقُوا۟ مِمَّا رَزَقَكُمُ ٱللَّهُ قَالَ ٱلَّذِينَ كَفَرُوا۟
لِلَّذِينَ ءَامَنُوٓا۟ أَنُطْعِمُ مَن لَّوْ يَشَآءُ ٱللَّهُ أَطْعَمَهُۥٓ إِنْ أَنتُمْ إِلَّا فِى
ضَلَٰلٍ مُّبِينٍ ﴿٤٧﴾ وَيَقُولُونَ مَتَىٰ هَٰذَا ٱلْوَعْدُ إِن كُنتُمْ صَٰدِقِينَ
﴿٤٨﴾ مَا يَنظُرُونَ إِلَّا صَيْحَةً وَٰحِدَةً تَأْخُذُهُمْ وَهُمْ يَخِصِّمُونَ
﴿٤٩﴾ فَلَا يَسْتَطِيعُونَ تَوْصِيَةً وَلَآ إِلَىٰٓ أَهْلِهِمْ يَرْجِعُونَ ﴿٥٠﴾

TRANSLATIONS

33. A Sign for them is the earth that is dead: We do give it life, and produce grain therefrom, of which you do eat.
34. And We produce therein orchards with date-palms and vines, and We cause springs to gush forth therein;

35. That they may enjoy {*akala*} the fruits of this (artistry): it was not their hands that made this: will they not then give thanks?
36. Glory to Allah, Who created in pairs all things that the earth produces, as well as their own (human) kind and (other)

33. A token unto them is the dead earth. We revive it, and We bring forth from it grain so that they eat thereof;
34. And We have placed therein gardens of the date palm and grapes, and We have caused springs of water to gush forth therein,
35. That they may eat of the fruit thereof and their hand made it not. Will they not, then, give thanks?

36. Glory be to Him Who created all the sexual pairs, of that which the earth groweth, and of themselves, and of that

things of which they have no knowledge.
37. And a Sign for them is the Night: We withdraw therefrom the Day, and behold they are plunged in darkness;
38. And the Sun runs its course for a period determined for it; that is the decree of (Him), the exalted in Might, the All-Knowing.
39. And the Moon - We have measured for it mansions (to traverse) till she returns like the old (and withered) lower part of date-stalk (*'urjūn*).
40. It is not permitted to the Sun to catch up the Moon, nor can the Night outstrip the Day: each (just) swims along in (its own) orbit (according to Law).
41. And a Sign for them is that We bore their race (through the flood) in the loaded Ark;
42. And We have created for them similar (vessels) on which they ride.
43. If it were Our Will, We could drown them: then would there be no helper (to hear their cry), nor could they be delivered.
44. Except by way of Mercy from Us, and by way of (worldly) convenience (to serve them) for a time.
45. When they are told, "Fear you that which is before you and that which will be after you, in order that you may receive Mercy," (they turn back).
46. Not a Sign comes to them from among the Signs of their Lord, but they turn away therefrom.

which they know not!
37. A token unto them is night. We strip it of the day, and lo! they are in darkness:
38. And the sun runs on unto a resting-place for him. That is the measuring of the Mighty, the Wise.
39. And for the moon We have appointed mansions till she return like an old shriveled palm-leaf.
40. It is not for the sun to overtake the moon, nor does the night outstrip the day. They float each in an orbit.
41. And a token unto them is that We bear their offspring in the laden ship,
42. And have created for them of the like thereof whereon they ride.
43. And if We will, We drown them, and there is no help for them, neither can they be saved;
44. Unless by mercy from Us and as comfort for a while.
45. When it is said unto them: Beware of that which is before you and that which is behind you, that haply {by chance) you may find mercy (they are heedless).
46. Never came a token of the tokens of their Lord to them, but they did turn away from it!

47. And when they are told, "Spend you of (the bounties) with which Allāh has provided you." The Unbelievers say to those who believe: "Shall we then feed those whom, if Allāh had so willed, He would have fed, (himself)? - you are in nothing but manifest error."

48. Further, they say, "When will this promise (come to pass), if what you say is true?"

49. They will not (have to) wait for aught but a single Blast: it will seize them while they are yet disputing among themselves!

50. No (chance) will they then have, by will, to dispose (of their affairs), nor to return to their own people!

(A. Y. Ali)

47. And when it is said unto them: Spend of that wherewith Allah has provided you, those who disbelieve say unto those who believe, Shall we feed those whom Allah, if He willed, would feed? You are in naught else than error manifest.

48. And they say: When will this promise be fulfilled, if you are truthful?

49. They await but one Shout, which will surprise them while they are disputing.

50. Then they cannot make bequest, nor can they return to their own folk.

(M. M. Pickthal)

EXPLANATION (A. Y. Ali, revised)

33: In the event that one may ask, "If they are destroyed, how can they be brought before the Judgement seat?", think about this: the earth is, in all practicality, dead in the Winter, and Allāh ﷻ revives it in the Spring. Similarly, when people die, Allāh ﷻ will revive them on the Day of Judgement.

34: All that is necessary for food and satisfaction is produced from what appears as lifeless soil, fertilized by rain and springs. Here is wonderful evidence of the power of Allāh ﷻ.

35: Literally, 'eat' (*akala)*. A broad meaning of profit, satisfaction, and enjoyment may be attached to the word "eat" in verse 33 above.
Humans may till the soil and sow the seed, but the productive forces of nature were not made by human hands. They are the handiwork and artistry of Allāh ﷻ.

36: The mystery of the two sexes, male and female, runs through all creation: in man, in animal, in vegetation, and possibly in other things of which we have no knowledge. Furthermore, there are pairs of opposite forces in nature, e.g., positive and negative electricity, etc. The atom itself consists of a positively charged nucleus or proton, surrounded by negatively charged electrons. Thus, constitution of matter itself is referred to as pairs of opposite energies.

37: "Withdrawing the Day from the Night" is a striking phrase and very appropriate. This whole section deals with signs or symbols, things in the physical world around us, from which we can learn the deepest spiritual truths if we sincerely apply ourselves to them.

38: *Mustaqarr* may mean:

(1) a limit of time; a determined period

(2) a place of rest

(3) a dwelling place

I believe that the first meaning is most applicable here, but some commentators adopt the second meaning. In that case, the simile would be that of the sun running its course in the daytime while it is visible to us, and resting during the night to prepare itself for its course the following day.

39: The lunar stations are the 28 divisions of the Zodiac, which are supposed to mark the daily course of the moon in the heavens, from the onset of the new moon to the time when the moon fades away.
'Urjūn: a raceme of dates or of a date-palm; or the base or lower part of the raceme. When it becomes old, it appears yellow, dry, and withered, and curved like a sickle; hence the comparison with the sickle-like appearance of the new moon.

40: Though the sun and the moon both cross the belt of the Zodiac, their courses are different. They never catch up with each other. When the sun and the moon are on the same side, in line with the earth, a solar eclipse occurs. When they are on opposite sides in a line, a lunar eclipse occurs, but there is no clash. Their laws are fixed by Allāh ﷻ, and form the subject of study in astronomy.
How beautifully the rounded courses of the planets and heavenly bodies are described, "swimming" through space, with perfectly smooth motions!

41: This is a reference to the story of Prophet Noah ﷺ and the Flood, which is symbolic of Allāh's Justice and Mercy. Prophet Noah's Ark was a "Sign to all People" (*Al-`Ankabūt* 29:15). Humankind's own personal experience is appealed to in every ship afloat: see next note.

42: The stately ships sailing through the seas would cover all kinds of seacraft as well as modern aircraft. The aircraft "swims" through air as ships do through water.

43: If Allāh ﷻ did not give human beings the intelligence to construct and manage seacraft and aircraft, the natural laws of gravity would lead to their destruction. It is the gift (mercy) of Allāh ﷻ that saves them.

44: Allāh ﷻ has blessed humankind with all these wonders of nature. Had it not been for these gifts, human life would face grave dangers at sea, land, or in the air. One should not regard the enjoyment of these conveniences as eternal: they are only given for a time in this life.

45: Humans should consider the consequences of their past actions, and guard against these consequences in their future actions. However, this logic does not satisfy those who prefer this worldly life to the *'Ākhirah*. They are bored with moral preaching, and turn away from it, to their own loss.

46: The Signs of Allāh ﷻ are many: in His great world, in nature, in the heart of human, and in the Revelation sent through His messengers. They turn away from all of these Signs, just as a human who has ruined his eyesight turns away from the light.

47: To selfish people, the good people may make an appeal, and say: "Look! Allāh ﷻ has given you wealth (or influence, or knowledge, or talent). Why not spend some of it in charity?" But the selfish only think of themselves and laugh at such ideas. They are too arrogant to find a place in their hearts for others. They say, "If Allāh ﷻ gave them nothing, why should we?" There is arrogance in this as well as disbelief: arrogance in thinking that they are favored because of their merits, and disbelief in laying the blame for other people's misfortunes on Allāh ﷻ.

48-50: In addition to their arrogance, they refuse Faith and ridicule the People of Faith: "If there is a Hereafter, tell us when it will be!" The answer is: "It will come sooner than you expect. You will be disputing about things of Faith and neglecting your opportunities in life, when the Hour will sound, and you will have no time even to make a will in this life. You will be cut off from everyone you thought to be near and dear to you, and no one will be able to help you!"

IMPORTANT POINTS TO LEARN AND REFLECT UPON

- There are many signs of Allāh ﷻ in heaven and on earth for a thinking person to reflect upon.
- The non-believers reject Allāh's Signs and His commands, but to their own peril.
- Out of mischief, they demand the coming of Judgement Day, which will surely come with a suddenness that they can never imagine.

GLOSSARY WORDS

akala, *`urjūn*, consequence, lunar, solar

VOCABULARY

الركوع ٣ - Section 3

بِسْمِ ٱللَّهِ ٱلرَّحْمَٰنِ ٱلرَّحِيمِ

(٣٣) وَ ءَايَةٌ لَّهُمُ	A Sign for them	(٣٤) وَجَعَلْنَا فِيهَا	And we produce therein
ٱلْأَرْضُ	the earth	جَنَّٰتٍ	orchards, gardens
ٱلْمَيْتَةُ	that is dead	مِّن نَّخِيلٍ	with date palms
أَحْيَيْنَٰهَا	We do give it life	وَ أَعْنَٰبٍ	and vines
وَ أَخْرَجْنَا	and We produce	وَ فَجَّرْنَا	and We cause to gush forth
مِنْهَا حَبًّا	grain thereform	فِيهَا	therein
فَمِنْهُ يَأْكُلُونَ	of which they do eat	مِنَ ٱلْعُيُونِ	the springs

لِيَأْكُلُوا (٣٥)	That they may enjoy, eat	ذٰلِكَ تَقْدِيرُ	that is the decree of (Him)
مِنْ ثَمَرِهِ	from the fruits	الْعَزِيزِ	the Exalted in Might
وَمَا عَمِلَتْهُ	It was not that made this	الْعَلِيمِ	the all-Knowing
أَيْدِيهِمْ	their hands	وَ الْقَمَرَ (٣٩)	And the moon
أَفَلَا يَشْكُرُونَ	will they not then give thanks	قَدَّرْنٰهُ	We have measured for it
سُبْحٰنَ (٣٦)	Glory to Allah	مَنَازِلَ	mansions (to traverse)
الَّذِى خَلَقَ الْأَزْوٰجَ	Who created in pairs	حَتّٰى عَادَ	till it returns
كُلَّهَا	all things	كَالْعُرْجُونِ	like lower part of a date stalk
مِمَّا تُنْبِتُ الْأَرْضُ	that the earth produces	الْقَدِيمِ	the old
وَمِنْ أَنْفُسِهِمْ	as well as their own kind	لَا الشَّمْسُ (٤٠)	It is not the sun
وَمِمَّا	and things of which	يَنْبَغِى لَهَآ	permitted to
لَا يَعْلَمُونَ	they have no knowledge	أَنْ تُدْرِكَ الْقَمَرَ	to catch up the moon
وَ ءَايَةٌ لَّهُمُ (٣٧)	And a Sign for them	وَ لَا الَّيْلُ	nor can the night
الَّيْلُ	the night	سَابِقُ النَّهَارِ	outstrip the day
نَسْلَخُ	We withdraw	وَكُلٌّ فِى فَلَكٍ	each in (his own) orbit
مِنْهُ النَّهَارَ	therefrom the day	يَسْبَحُونَ	swims along
فَإِذَاهُمْ	and behold	وَ ءَايَةٌ لَّهُمْ (٤١)	And a Sign for them
مُظْلِمُونَ	they are plunged in to darkness	أَنَّا حَمَلْنَا	that We bore
وَ الشَّمْسُ (٣٨)	And the sun	ذُرِّيَّتَهُمْ	their race (through the flood)
تَجْرِى	runs its course	فِى الْفُلْكِ	in the ark
لِمُسْتَقَرٍّ لَهَا	for a period determined for it	الْمَشْحُونِ	loaded

(٤٢) وَخَلَقْنَا لَهُمْ	And We have created for them
مِّنْ مِّثْلِهِ	similar (vessels)
مَا يَرْكَبُونَ	on which they ride
(٤٣) وَ إِنْ نَّشَأْ	If it were Our Will
نُغْرِقْهُمْ	We could drown them
فَلاَ	then would there be no one
صَرِيخَ لَهُمْ	to hear their cry
وَ لاَ هُمْ يُنْقَذُونَ	nor could they be delivered
(٤٤) إِلاَّ رَحْمَةً	Except through Mercy
مِّنَّا	from Us
وَمَتَاعًا	and by way of convenience
إِلَىٰ حِينٍ	for a time
(٤٥) وَ إِذَا قِيلَ لَهُمُ	When they are told
اتَّقُوا	fear you
مَا بَيْنَ أَيْدِيكُمْ	that which is before you
وَمَا	and that which will be
خَلْفَكُمْ	after you
لَعَلَّكُمْ	in order that
تُرْحَمُونَ	you may receive Mercy
(٤٦) وَمَا تَأْتِيهِمْ	And does not come to them
مِّنْ ءَايَةٍ	a Sign

مِّنْ ءَايَٰتِ	from among the Signs
رَبِّهِمْ	of their Lord
إِلاَّ كَانُوا	but they
عَنْهَا مُعْرِضِينَ	turn away therefrom
(٤٧) وَ إِذَا قِيلَ لَهُمْ	And when they are told
أَنْفِقُوا	spend you of (the bounties)
مِمَّا	with which
رَزَقَكُمُ اللهُ	Allah has provided you
قَالَ الَّذِينَ كَفَرُوا	the unbelievers say
لِلَّذِينَ ءَامَنُوٓا	to those who believe
أَنُطْعِمُ	shall we then feed
مَنْ لَّوْ	those whom if
يَشَآءُ اللهُ	Allah had so willed
أَطْعَمَهُۥ	He would have fed
إِنْ أَنْتُمْ إِلاَّ	you are in nothing but
فِى ضَلَٰلٍ مُّبِينٍ	a manifest error
(٤٨) وَ يَقُولُونَ	And they say
مَتَىٰ	when will
هَٰذَا الْوَعْدُ	this promise (come to pass)
إِنْ كُنْتُمْ	if what you say
صَٰدِقِينَ	is true

(٤٩) مَا يَنْظُرُونَ	They will not wait for aught	(٥٠) فَلاَ يَسْتَطِيعُونَ	No (chance) will they have
إِلاَّ صَيْحَةً وَاحِدَةً	but a single blast	تَوْصِيَةً	to make a will
تَأْخُذُهُمْ	It will seize them	وَلاَ إِلَىٰ	nor to
وَهُمْ	while they are yet	أَهْلِهِمْ	their own people
يَخِصِّمُونَ	disputing among themselves	يَرْجِعُونَ	to return

Section 4: 51-67

SŪRAH YĀ-SĪN 36

Yā Sīn / Yā Sīn

ARABIC TEXT

بِسۡمِ ٱللَّهِ ٱلرَّحۡمَٰنِ ٱلرَّحِيمِ

وَنُفِخَ فِي ٱلصُّورِ فَإِذَا هُم مِّنَ ٱلۡأَجۡدَاثِ إِلَىٰ رَبِّهِمۡ يَنسِلُونَ
(٥١) قَالُواْ يَٰوَيۡلَنَا مَنۢ بَعَثَنَا مِن مَّرۡقَدِنَاۜۗ هَٰذَا مَا وَعَدَ ٱلرَّحۡمَٰنُ
وَصَدَقَ ٱلۡمُرۡسَلُونَ (٥٢) إِن كَانَتۡ إِلَّا صَيۡحَةٗ
وَٰحِدَةٗ فَإِذَا هُمۡ جَمِيعٞ لَّدَيۡنَا مُحۡضَرُونَ (٥٣) فَٱلۡيَوۡمَ لَا تُظۡلَمُ
نَفۡسٞ شَيۡـٔٗا وَلَا تُجۡزَوۡنَ إِلَّا مَا كُنتُمۡ تَعۡمَلُونَ (٥٤)
إِنَّ أَصۡحَٰبَ ٱلۡجَنَّةِ ٱلۡيَوۡمَ فِي شُغُلٖ فَٰكِهُونَ (٥٥) هُمۡ وَأَزۡوَٰجُهُمۡ
فِي ظِلَٰلٍ عَلَى ٱلۡأَرَآئِكِ مُتَّكِـُٔونَ (٥٦) لَهُمۡ فِيهَا فَٰكِهَةٞ وَلَهُم
مَّا يَدَّعُونَ (٥٧) سَلَٰمٞ قَوۡلٗا مِّن رَّبّٖ رَّحِيمٖ (٥٨) وَٱمۡتَٰزُواْ ٱلۡيَوۡمَ
أَيُّهَا ٱلۡمُجۡرِمُونَ (٥٩) ۞ أَلَمۡ أَعۡهَدۡ إِلَيۡكُمۡ يَٰبَنِيٓ ءَادَمَ أَن لَّا
تَعۡبُدُواْ ٱلشَّيۡطَٰنَۖ إِنَّهُۥ لَكُمۡ عَدُوّٞ مُّبِينٞ (٦٠) وَأَنِ ٱعۡبُدُونِيۚ
هَٰذَا صِرَٰطٞ مُّسۡتَقِيمٞ (٦١) وَلَقَدۡ أَضَلَّ مِنكُمۡ جِبِلّٗا كَثِيرًاۖ
أَفَلَمۡ تَكُونُواْ تَعۡقِلُونَ (٦٢) هَٰذِهِۦ جَهَنَّمُ ٱلَّتِي كُنتُمۡ تُوعَدُونَ
(٦٣) ٱصۡلَوۡهَا ٱلۡيَوۡمَ بِمَا كُنتُمۡ تَكۡفُرُونَ (٦٤) ٱلۡيَوۡمَ نَخۡتِمُ

عَلَىٰٓ أَفْوَٰهِهِمْ وَتُكَلِّمُنَآ أَيْدِيهِمْ وَتَشْهَدُ أَرْجُلُهُم بِمَا كَانُوا۟
يَكْسِبُونَ ﴿٦٥﴾ وَلَوْ نَشَآءُ لَطَمَسْنَا عَلَىٰٓ أَعْيُنِهِمْ فَٱسْتَبَقُوا۟
ٱلصِّرَٰطَ فَأَنَّىٰ يُبْصِرُونَ ﴿٦٦﴾ وَلَوْ نَشَآءُ لَمَسَخْنَٰهُمْ
عَلَىٰ مَكَانَتِهِمْ فَمَا ٱسْتَطَٰعُوا۟ مُضِيًّا وَلَا يَرْجِعُونَ ﴿٦٧﴾

TRANSLATIONS

51. The trumpet shall be sounded, when behold! from the sepulchers (men) will rush forth to their Lord!

52. They will say: "Ah! woe unto us! Who has raised us up from our beds of repose?" (A voice will say:) "This is what (Allāh) Most Gracious had promised, and true was the word of the messengers!"

53. It will be no more than a single Blast, when lo! they will all be brought up before Us!

54. Then, on that Day, not a soul will be wronged in the least, and you shall but be repaid the meeds of your past Deeds.

55. Verily the Companions of the Garden shall that Day have joy in all that they do;

56. They and their associates will be in groves of (cool) shade, reclining on thrones (of dignity);

51. And the trumpet is blown and lo! from the graves they hie {rush} unto their Lord,

52. Crying: Woe upon us! Who has raised us from our place of sleep? This is that which the Beneficent did promise, and the messengers spoke truth.

53. It is but one Shout, and behold them brought together before Us!

54. This day no soul is wronged in aught; nor are you requited aught but what you used to do.

55. Lo! those who merit Paradise this day are happily employed,

56. They and their wives, in pleasant shade, on thrones reclining;

57. (Every) fruit (enjoyment) will be there for them; they shall have whatever they call for;
58. "Peace!"- a Word (of salutation) from a Lord Most Merciful!
59. And O you in sin! Get you apart this Day!
60. "Did I not enjoin on you, O you children of Adam, that you should not worship Satan; for that he was to you an enemy avowed? -
61. "And that you should worship Me, (for that) this was the Straight Way?
62. "But he did lead astray a great multitude of you. Did you not, then, understand?
63. "This is the Hell of which you were (repeatedly) warned!
64. "Embrace you the (Fire) this Day, for that you (persistently) rejected (Truth)."
65. That Day shall We set a seal on their mouths. But their hands will speak to Us, and their feet bear witness, to all that they did.
66. If it had been Our Will, We could surely have blotted out their eyes; then should they have run about groping for the Path, but how could they have seen?
67. And if it had been Our Will, We could have transformed them (to remain) in their places; then should they have been unable to move about, nor could they have returned (after error).

(A. Y. Ali)

57. Theirs the fruit (of their good deeds) and theirs (all) that they ask;

58. The word from a Merciful Lord (for them) is: Peace!
59. But avaunt you, O you guilty, this day!
60. Did I not charge you, O you sons of Adam, that you worship not the devil - Lo! he is your open foe!-

61. But that you worship Me? That was the right path.
62. Yet he has led astray of you a great multitude. Had you then no sense?

63. This is hell which you were promised (if you followed him).
64. Burn therein this day for that you disbelieved.
65. This day We seal up mouths, and hands speak out and feet bear witness as to what they used to earn.

66. And had We willed, We verily could have quenched their eyesight so that they should struggle for the way. Then how could they have seen?
67. And had We willed, We verily could have fixed them in their place, making them powerless to go forward or turn back.

(M. M. Pickthal)

EXPLANATION (A. Y. Ali, revised)

51: According to tradition, the angel who will sound the Trumpet {*aṣ-Ṣūr*} is Isrāfīl, but the name does not occur in the Qur'ān. The Trumpet, which will announce the end of this world, is mentioned in many places in the Qur'ān.

52: The dead will arise in confusion and will be reminded that Allāh ﷻ, in His Grace and Mercy, has already announced the Hereafter. The words of Allāh's messengers, which then seemed so strange, were true and their predictions are now being fulfilled!

53: Time and Space, as we know them, will be no more. The whole gathering will occur in a blink of an eye.

54: The Judgement will be on the highest standard of Divine Justice and Grace. Even the least merit will be rewarded generously. No penalty will be given, except that which the doer brought on himself by his past deeds.

55: It will be *Jannah*, a Garden, everything agreeable to see, hear, feel, taste, and smell. The joy in the Garden will be unending: everything we do will be a source of pure joy without sorrow.

56: Secondly, this joy or happiness will be shared between spouses.

57: Thirdly, aside from external Bliss, their happiness will be from within: a true feeling of fulfillment and contentment in the Hereafter.

58: Fourthly, we reach the highest grade of bliss, the salutation "Peace!" from Allāh, Most Merciful Himself. That word sums up the attainment of the final Goal. It explains the nature of the Most High: He is not only a Lord and Cherisher, but a Lord Whose supreme glory is Mercy and Peace!

59: Notice how this finely balanced passage reaches the height of peace in describing the state of the Blessed, in the word *Salām*. It then gradually takes us down to think about the state of the sinners.

It refers to their negative state of isolation. On this Day of Judgement, they will not be given the chance to be with the Blessed and share in their spiritual profits. The first feature of the Day of Judgement is that it is a Day of Separation; of sorting out. Each soul will now find its own true level in accordance with their past deeds.

60: There is a gentle criticism of the wrong-doers. They are addressed as "children of Adam" to emphasize two facts:

(1) They have disgraced their ancestry. After his fall, Adam ﷺ repented and was forgiven. The destiny of humankind has been the prize open to all of his descendants

(2) Throughout the ages, Allāh, Most Merciful, has continued to warn humankind against the traps laid by Satan, the avowed enemy of humans.

61: Besides the warning, the straight Way was shown to them: the Way of those who receive Allāh's Grace and attain happiness.

62: Allāh ﷻ points out that they were given understanding (*'aql*), so that by their own minds, they could have judged their own best interests. Yet, they misused their ability to reason, and deliberately threw away their chance! And not only a few, but so many!

63: The final consequences of their actions are now placed before them, the Hellfire: the state of condemnation, which they could so easily have avoided!

64: As they deliberately rejected all teachings, guidance, and warnings, they are now told to experience the Fire of Punishment, for it is simply the consequence of their own doing.

65: The disbelievers will be unable to defend their actions. Their silence will not matter. Their own hands and feet will speak against them. "Hands and feet" in this connection are symbolic of all the human organs which they were given in this life. The same extended meaning is to be applied to "eyes" in the following verse.

66: "If it had been Our Will" i.e., if such had been the Will and Plan of Allāh ﷻ. If Allāh ﷻ had not intended to give us our limited free will or power of choice, the case would have been different; there would have been no moral responsibility to enforce.

67: If Allāh's Plan had been not to grant unlimited freedom of choice or will to humankind, He could have created us quite differently. He also could have transformed us into stationary creatures lacking moral or spiritual qualities, and there would be no possibility of progress or deterioration. Humans would then have been unable to reach the spiritual heights now open to us. It would not be possible for us to return through the door of *Tawbah* (repentance) and to God's favor. However, it was Allāh's Plan to give us the freedom of choice, and we must shoulder all the responsibilities that go with these choices.

IMPORTANT POINTS TO LEARN AND REFLECT UPON

- On the Day of Judgement, everyone will be resurrected and brought to judgement.
- The People of *Jannah* (Garden) and their spouses will have all the pleasures there, and special greetings of *Salām* (Peace) from their Lord.
- The People of the Fire will be separated from the People of *Jannah* and sent to their punishment because of their evil deeds.

GLOSSARY WORDS

deterioration, repentance, Cherisher, *Salām*, *Tawbah*

VOCABULARY

الركوع ٤ - Section 4

بِسْمِ ٱللَّهِ ٱلرَّحْمَٰنِ ٱلرَّحِيمِ

(٥١) وَنُفِخَ فِى الصُّورِ	The trumpet shall be sounded	مِنْ مَّرْقَدِنَا	from our beds of repose
فَإِذَا هُمْ	when behold	هَٰذَا مَا وَعَدَ	this is what had promised
مِّنَ الْأَجْدَاثِ	from the sepulchres	الرَّحْمَٰنُ	the Most Gracious
إِلَىٰ رَبِّهِمْ	to their Lord	وَصَدَقَ الْمُرْسَلُونَ	and true was the word
يَنْسِلُونَ	will rush forth	(٥٣) إِنْ كَانَتْ	It will be no more
(٥٢) قَالُوا يَٰوَيْلَنَا	They will say woe unto us	إِلَّا صَيْحَةً وَٰحِدَةً	than a single Blast
مَنْ بَعَثَنَا	who has raised us up	فَإِذَا هُمْ جَمِيعٌ	when lo they will all

لَدَيْنَا مُحْضَرُونَ	be brought up before Us
(٥٤) فَالْيَوْمَ	Then, on that Day
لَا تُظْلَمُ نَفْسٌ	not a soul will be wronged
شَيْئًا	in the least
وَ لَا تُجْزَوْنَ	and you shall not be paid
إِلَّا مَا كُنْتُمْ تَعْمَلُونَ	except for what you did
(٥٥) إِنَّ أَصْحٰبَ الْجَنَّةِ	Verily the Companions of the Garden
الْيَوْمَ	that Day
فِي شُغُلٍ	in all that they do
فٰكِهُونَ	have joy
(٥٦) هُمْ وَ أَزْوَاجُهُمْ	They and their spouses
فِي ظِلَٰلٍ	will be in groves of shade
عَلَى الْأَرَآئِكِ	on thrones (of dignity)
مُتَّكِئُونَ	reclining
(٥٧) لَهُمْ فِيهَا	Will be there for them
فَاكِهَةٌ	every fruit
وَ لَهُمْ مَا يَدَّعُونَ	they shall have whatever they call for
(٥٨) سَلٰمٌ قَوْلاً	Peace, a word
مِنْ رَبٍّ رَحِيمٍ	from a Lord, Most Merciful

(٥٩) وَ امْتَازُوا الْيَوْمَ	Be seperated this Day
أَيُّهَا الْمُجْرِمُونَ	O you sinners
(٦٠) أَلَمْ أَعْهَدْ إِلَيْكُمْ	Did I not enjoin on you
يٰبَنِيٓ اٰدَمَ	O children of Adam
أَنْ لَّا تَعْبُدُوا	that you should not worship
الشَّيْطٰنَ	the Satan
إِنَّهُ لَكُمْ	for that he was to you
عَدُوٌّ مُّبِينٌ	an enemy avowed
(٦١) وَ أَنِ	And that you should
اعْبُدُونِي	worship Me
هٰذَا صِرَاطٌ مُّسْتَقِيمٌ	this was the straight way
(٦٢) وَ لَقَدْ أَضَلَّ	But he did lead astray
مِنْكُمْ	from among you
جِبِلًّا كَثِيرًا	a great multitude
أَفَلَمْ تَكُونُوا	did you not, then
تَعْقِلُونَ	understand
(٦٣) هٰذِهِ جَهَنَّمُ	This is the Hell
الَّتِي كُنْتُمْ تُوعَدُونَ	of which you were warned
(٦٤) إِصْلَوْهَا	Burn you (the fire)
الْيَوْمَ	this Day
بِمَا كُنْتُمْ تَكْفُرُونَ	for that you rejected (the truth)

(٦٥) أَلْيَوْمَ نَخْتِمُ	That Day shall We set a seal
عَلَىٰٓ أَفْوَاهِهِمْ	on their mouths
وَ تُكَلِّمُنَآ أَيْدِيهِمْ	but their hands will speak to Us
وَ تَشْهَدُ أَرْجُلُهُمْ	and their feet bear witness
بِمَا كَانُوا يَكْسِبُونَ	that they did
(٦٦) وَ لَوْ نَشَآءُ	If it had been Our Will
لَطَمَسْنَا	We could surely have blotted out
عَلَىٰٓ أَعْيُنِهِمْ	their eyes

وَ تَشْهَدُ أَرْجُلُهُمْ	and their feet bear witness
بِمَا كَانُوا يَكْسِبُونَ	that they did
(٦٧) وَ لَوْ نَشَآءُ	And if it had been Our Will
لَمَسَخْنَٰهُمْ	We could have transformed them
عَلَىٰ مَكَانَتِهِمْ	in their places
فَمَا اسْتَطَاعُوا	then should they have been unable
مُضِيًّا	to move about
وَ لَا يَرْجِعُونَ	nor could they have returned

Section 5: 68-83

SŪRAH YĀ-SĪN 36

Yā Sīn / Yā Sīn

ARABIC TEXT

بِسْمِ اللَّهِ الرَّحْمَٰنِ الرَّحِيمِ

وَمَن نُّعَمِّرْهُ نُنَكِّسْهُ فِي الْخَلْقِ ۖ أَفَلَا يَعْقِلُونَ ﴿٦٨﴾
وَمَا عَلَّمْنَاهُ الشِّعْرَ وَمَا يَنبَغِي لَهُ ۚ إِنْ هُوَ إِلَّا ذِكْرٌ وَقُرْآنٌ مُّبِينٌ
﴿٦٩﴾ لِّيُنذِرَ مَن كَانَ حَيًّا وَيَحِقَّ الْقَوْلُ عَلَى الْكَافِرِينَ ﴿٧٠﴾
أَوَلَمْ يَرَوْا أَنَّا خَلَقْنَا لَهُم مِّمَّا عَمِلَتْ أَيْدِينَا أَنْعَامًا فَهُمْ لَهَا
مَالِكُونَ ﴿٧١﴾ وَذَلَّلْنَاهَا لَهُمْ فَمِنْهَا رَكُوبُهُمْ وَمِنْهَا يَأْكُلُونَ ﴿٧٢﴾
وَلَهُمْ فِيهَا مَنَافِعُ وَمَشَارِبُ ۖ أَفَلَا يَشْكُرُونَ ﴿٧٣﴾ وَاتَّخَذُوا
مِن دُونِ اللَّهِ آلِهَةً لَّعَلَّهُمْ يُنصَرُونَ ﴿٧٤﴾ لَا يَسْتَطِيعُونَ
نَصْرَهُمْ وَهُمْ لَهُمْ جُندٌ مُّحْضَرُونَ ﴿٧٥﴾ فَلَا يَحْزُنكَ قَوْلُهُمْ
إِنَّا نَعْلَمُ مَا يُسِرُّونَ وَمَا يُعْلِنُونَ ﴿٧٦﴾ أَوَلَمْ يَرَ الْإِنسَانُ أَنَّا
خَلَقْنَاهُ مِن نُّطْفَةٍ فَإِذَا هُوَ خَصِيمٌ مُّبِينٌ ﴿٧٧﴾ وَضَرَبَ لَنَا
مَثَلًا وَنَسِيَ خَلْقَهُ ۖ قَالَ مَن يُحْيِي الْعِظَامَ وَهِيَ رَمِيمٌ ﴿٧٨﴾
قُلْ يُحْيِيهَا الَّذِي أَنشَأَهَا أَوَّلَ مَرَّةٍ ۖ وَهُوَ بِكُلِّ خَلْقٍ عَلِيمٌ

﴿٧٩﴾ ٱلَّذِى جَعَلَ لَكُم مِّنَ ٱلشَّجَرِ ٱلْأَخْضَرِ نَارًا فَإِذَآ أَنتُم
مِّنْهُ تُوقِدُونَ ﴿٨٠﴾ أَوَلَيْسَ ٱلَّذِى خَلَقَ ٱلسَّمَٰوَٰتِ وَٱلْأَرْضَ
بِقَٰدِرٍ عَلَىٰٓ أَن يَخْلُقَ مِثْلَهُم ۚ بَلَىٰ وَهُوَ ٱلْخَلَّٰقُ ٱلْعَلِيمُ ﴿٨١﴾
إِنَّمَآ أَمْرُهُۥٓ إِذَآ أَرَادَ شَيْـًٔا أَن يَقُولَ لَهُۥ كُن فَيَكُونُ ﴿٨٢﴾
فَسُبْحَٰنَ ٱلَّذِى بِيَدِهِۦ مَلَكُوتُ كُلِّ شَىْءٍ وَإِلَيْهِ تُرْجَعُونَ ﴿٨٣﴾

TRANSLATIONS

68. If We grant long life to any, We cause him to be reversed in nature: will they not then understand?

69. We have not instructed the (Prophet) in Poetry *{ash-Shi'r}*, nor is it meet for him: this is no less than a Message and a Qur'ān making things clear:

70. That it may give admonition to any (who are) alive, and that the charge may be proved against those who reject (Truth).

71. See they not that it is We Who have created for them - among the things which Our hands have fashioned - cattle, which are under their dominion? -

72. And that We have subjected them to their (use)? Of them some do carry them and some they eat:

73. And they have (other) profits from

68. He whom We bring unto old age, We reverse him in creation (making him go back to weakness after strength). Have you then no sense?

69. And we have not taught him (Muhammad) poetry, nor is it meet for him. This is naught else than a Reminder and a Lecture making plain,

70. To warn whosoever lives, and that the word may be fulfilled against the disbelievers.

71. Have they not seen how We have created for them of Our handiwork the cattle, so that they are their owners,

72. And have subdued them unto them, so that some of them they have for riding, some for food?

73. Benefits and (divers) drinks have they

them (besides),and they get (milk) to drink. Will they not then be grateful?

74. Yet they take (for worship) gods other than Allāh, (hoping) that they might be helped!

75. They have not the power to help them: but they will be brought up (before Our Judgement Seat) as a troop (to be condemned).

76. Let not their speech, then, grieve you. Verily We know what they hide as well as what they disclose.

77. Does not human see that it is We Who created him from sperm? Yet behold! He (stands forth) as an open adversary!

78. And he makes comparisons for Us and forgets his own (Origin and) Creation: He says, "Who can give life to (dry) bones and decomposed ones (at that)?"

79. Say, "He will give them life Who created them for the first time! For He is well-versed in every kind of creation! -

80. "The same Who produces for you fire out of the green tree, when behold! You kindle therewith (your own fires)!

81. "Is not He Who created the heavens and the earth able to create the like thereof?" - Yes, indeed! for He is the Creator Supreme {*Al-Khallāq*}, of Skill and Knowledge (Infinite) {*Al-'Alīm*}!

82. Verily, when He intends a thing, His command is, "Be," {*Kun*} and it is {*Fa-yakūn*}!

83. So glory to Him in Whose Hands is the dominion {*Malakūt*} of all things: and

from them. Will they not then give thanks?

74. And they have taken (other) gods beside Allāh, in order that they may be helped.

75. It is not in their power to help them; but they (the worshipers) are unto them a host in arms.

76. So let not their speech grieve you (O Muhammad). Lo! We know what they conceal and what proclaim.

77. Has not man seen that We have created him from a drop of seed? Yet lo! he is an open opponent.

78. And he has coined for Us a similitude, and has forgotten the fact of his creation, saying: Who will revive these bones when they have rotted away?

79. Say: He will revive them Who produced them at the first, for He is Knower of every creation,

80. Who has appointed for you fire from the green tree, and behold! you kindle from it.

81. Is not He Who created the heavens and the earth, Able to create the like of them? Yes, that He is! for He is the All-Wise Creator,

82. But His command, when He intends a thing, is only that he says unto it: Be! and it is.

83. Therefor glory be to Him in Whose Hands is the dominion over all things!

to Him will you be all brought back. *(A. Y. Ali)*	Unto Him you will be brought back. *(M. M. Pickthal)*

EXPLANATION (A. Y. Ali, revised)

68: Everything is possible for Allāh ﷻ. If you doubt how humans can be changed from their present nature, think of the changes that we undergo at different stages of our life: we pass from childhood to young adulthood to middle age and to old age. In extreme old age, a kind of second childhood overtakes a person. Allāh ﷻ granted us many opportunities and responsibilities in this life, before old age and death overtake us.

69: Here "Poetry" is used as meaning 'fairy tales,' things futile and false; whereas the Qur'ān is a practical guide, true and clear. (See also *a<u>sh</u>-<u>Sh</u>u 'arā'* 26:224 and note)

70: "Alive" both in English and Arabic means not only "having physical life" but also having all the active qualities which we associate with life. In religious language, those who are unresponsive to the reality of the spiritual message are no better than those who are dead. If people knowingly reject Truth and Faith after they have been warned, the charge of rebellion is proved against them. They cannot plead their ignorance.

71-73: If they are blind to the other Signs of Allāh ﷻ, they can at least ponder over the simple, everyday things by which they receive so many blessings. How is it that wild animals can be trained and made useful to humans? Humans can use them for riding or in times of drought; they can use their flesh for food and drink their milk; they can use their hair for wool. Their skins are used for leather, furs for warmth, sheep's wool or camel's hair for blankets or textiles, musk for perfume, and so on.

74: The whole argument of Allāh ﷻ focuses on this: 'Our teaching is for your own benefit. We provide all these blessings for you, and yet you turn away from Me, the Giver of all, and are busy pursuing your own foolish ideas!'

75: There is some difference of opinion among commentators as to the exact meaning of this clause. As I understand it, the meaning seems to be this: humans tend to forget or turn away from the true God, the source of all that is good, and they go after imaginary powers in the form of false gods, heroes, humans, or abstract things, (such as science or nature or philosophy) or superstitious things (such as Magic, or Good-Fortune or Ill-Fortune, or one's own selfish desires). Such a person believes that these things will help him in this Life or in the Hereafter (if he even believes in a Hereafter), but in fact, they cannot help him. On the contrary, all things that are false will be brought up and condemned by Allāh ﷻ on the Day of Judgement, and the worshippers of these superficial things will also be treated as people worthy of condemnation. Thus instead of helping them, the falsehoods will only serve to further condemn them on the Day of Judgement.

76: If some people are so foolish as to reject Allāh ﷻ, let not the People of Allāh ﷻ (the Beleivers) grieve over it. They should do their duty and leave the rest to Him. His Plan will ultimately prevail.

77: Human disobedience and folly are all the more surprising, given the fact that without Allāh's Greatness and Mercy, human beings are such insignificant creatures, created out of something that is less than a drop in the vast ocean of existence. Yet, humans obstinately dispute with their Maker, and make comparisons of Him and His creation, as in the next verse!

78: That is, humans think that Allāh ﷻ is like His creatures. Yet, Allāh ﷻ asks: 'Who can give life to dry (and decomposed) bones?' None of Allāh's creatures can perform such a miracle. How can one compare the limited power of Allāh's creatures with His power as the Creator of all things, including ourselves? Indeed, the first creation out of nothing is far more difficult for us to imagine than subsequent re-creation.

79: Allāh's creative artistry is evident in every phase of nature, and it is operating continuously at every moment in time. The more humans begin to understand themselves and the things within their reach, the more they will realize this fact. How naive it is of anyone to set imaginary limits on Allāh's powers. There are more ways of creation than we, with our limited imaginations, can dream of!

80: {The green wood, the plants and the trees containing water have the hidden power to burn, create fire and produce energy. A.G.}

81: Which is more difficult to create: the human being, or the heavens and the earth, with all their limitless creatures? Allāh ﷻ created the heavens and the earth, with all their creatures, and He can create other worlds just like those. Thus, for Him, it is a small matter to raise us in the Hereafter.

82: And His creation is not dependent on time, or instruments, or means, or any other condition whatsoever. Existence awaits His Will, or Plan, or Intention. The moment He Wills a thing, it becomes. Only His Word or Command is needed, and the thing comes into existence.

83: All things have been created and maintained by Allāh ﷻ and will eventually return to Him. The point of special interest to us is that *we* will also be brought back to Allāh ﷻ. We are answerable to Him alone. This Message is the very essence of the Revelation; it explains the significance of the Hereafter; and it appropriately concludes a *Sūrah* especially connected with the name of the Prophet ﷺ *(Yā-Sīn)*.

IMPORTANT POINTS TO LEARN AND REFLECT UPON

- Rasūlullāh ﷺ was not a poet; he was a Prophet with a life-giving message.
- He was sent by the same Lord Who has created for us animals and other useful things.
- He created humans from nothing, and He will resurrect us again in the Hereafter.

GLOSSARY WORDS

Ash-Shi'r, Kun, Fa-yakūn, Malakūt, obstinacy, rebellion, transformation

VOCABULARY

الركوع ٥ - Section 5

بِسْمِ ٱللَّهِ ٱلرَّحْمَٰنِ ٱلرَّحِيمِ

(٦٨) وَ مَنْ نُعَمِّرْهُ	If We grant long life to any
نُنَكِّسْهُ	We cause him to be reversed
فِى الْخَلْقِ	in nature
أَفَلاَ يَعْقِلُونَ	will they not then understand
وَمَا عَلَّمْنَٰهُ	We have not taught him
اَلشِّعْرَ	the poetry
وَمَا يَنْبَغِى لَهُ	Nor is it suitable for him
إِنْ هُوَ إِلاَّ ذِكْرٌ	this is no less than a Message
وَّ قُرْاٰنٌ مُّبِينٌ	and a Qur'an making things clear
(٦٩) لِّيُنْذِرَ	That it may warn
مَنْ كَانَ حَيًّا	to any who are alive
(٧٠) وَّ يَحِقَّ الْقَوْلُ	And that the truth may be proved
عَلَى الْكٰفِرِينَ	against the disbelievers
(٧١) أَوَ لَمْ يَرَوْا	See they not that it is
أَنَّا خَلَقْنَا لَهُمْ	We Who have created for them
مِّمَّا عَمِلَتْ	the things which have fashioned
أَيْدِينَآ	Our Hands
أَنْعَامًا	cattle

فَهُمْ لَهَا مٰلِكُونَ	which are under their dominion
(٧٢) وَ ذَلَّلْنٰهَا	And We subjected them
لَهُمْ	to their use
فَمِنْهَا رَكُوبُهُمْ	of them some do carry them
وَمِنْهَا يَأْكُلُونَ	and some they eat
(٧٣) وَ لَهُمْ فِيهَا مَنَافِعُ	And they have other profits
وَمَشَارِبُ	and drink
أَفَلاَ يَشْكُرُونَ	will they not be grateful
(٧٤) وَ اتَّخَذُوا	They take
مِنْ دُونِ اللهِ اٰلِهَةً	gods other than Allah
لَّعَلَّهُمْ يُنْصَرُونَ	that they might be helped
(٧٥) لاَ يَسْتَطِيعُونَ	They have not the power
نَصْرَهُمْ	to help them
وَهُمْ لَهُمْ	but they will be brought up
جُنْدٌ مُّحْضَرُونَ	as a troop to be condemned
(٧٦) فَلاَ يَحْزُنْكَ	Let not then grieve thee
قَوْلُهُمْ	their speech
إِنَّا نَعْلَمُ	verily We know

وَمَا يُعْلِنُونَ	as well as what they disclose
(٧٧) أَوَ لَمْ يَرَ الْإِنْسَانُ	Does not human see
أَنَّا خَلَقْنَهُ	it is We Who created him
مِنْ نُّطْفَةٍ	from sperm
فَإِذَا هُوَ	yet behold he stands forth
خَصِيمٌ مُّبِينٌ	as an open adversary
(٧٨) وَضَرَبَ لَنَا	And he makes for Us
مَثَلاً	comparisons
وَّ نَسِيَ خَلْقَهُ	and forgets his own creation
قَالَ مَنْ	He says who can
يُحْيِ الْعِظَامَ	give life to bones
وَهِيَ رَمِيمٌ	and decomposed ones
(٧٩) قُلْ يُحْيِيهَا	Say, He will give them life
الَّذِيٓ أَنْشَأَهَآ	Who created them
أَوَّلَ مَرَّةٍ	for the first time
وَهُوَ بِكُلِّ	and He is of every kind
خَلْقٍ عَلِيمٌ	of creation knowledgeable
(٨٠) الَّذِي جَعَلَ لَكُمْ	The same who produces for you
مِّنَ الشَّجَرِ الْأَخْضَرِ	from the green tree
نَارًا	fire

فَإِذَآ أَنْتُمْ	when behold you
مِّنْهُ تُوقِدُونَ	kindle therewith
(٨١) أَوَ لَيْسَ الَّذِي	Is not He Who
خَلَقَ السَّمٰوٰتِ	created the heavens
وَ الْأَرْضَ	and the earth
بِقٰدِرٍ عَلٰٓى	able to
أَنْ يَّخْلُقَ	create thereof
مِثْلَهُمْ	the like
بَلٰى	Yes! indeed
وَهُوَ الْخَلّٰقُ	for He is the Creator
الْعَلِيمُ	with knowledge
(٨٢) إِنَّمَآ أَمْرُهُ	Verily, His command is
إِذَآ أَرَادَ شَيْئًا	when He intends a thing
أَنْ يَّقُولَ لَهُ	He says to it
كُنْ فَيَكُونُ	be! and it is
(٨٣) فَسُبْحٰنَ الَّذِي	So glory to Him
بِيَدِهِ	in Whose Hands is
مَلَكُوتُ	the dominion
كُلِّ شَيْءٍ	of all things
وَّ إِلَيْهِ	and to Him
تُرْجَعُونَ	will you all brought back

Section 1:1-25

سُورَةُ الرَّحْمَٰنِ

SŪRAH AR-RAḤMĀN 55: 1-78

The Most Gracious / The Beneficent

Name: This *Sūrah* is entitled *Ar-Raḥmān* (Most Gracious), one of the most popular Names of Allāh ﷻ, and with which the *Sūrah* begins. The title of *Ar-Raḥmān* describes Allāh's beautiful attributes of Mercy and Grace repeatedly throughout the *Sūrah.*

Period of Revelation: Most commentators hold the view that this is an early Makkan *Sūrah.* According to some traditions, it was revealed (at least some part of it) in Madīnah. Some reliable traditions establish it as a Makkan *Sūrah,* revealed many years before the *Hijrah.*
'Abdullah bin `Umar relates an incident in early Makkan life: once Rasūlullāh ﷺ recited *Sūrah Ar-Raḥmān* before his *Ṣaḥābah*. Then he said to the people: "How is it that I do not hear from you the good answer that the *jinn* had given to their Lord?"
The people asked the nature of the response of the *jinn.* He replied: "As I recited the Divine Words, *Fa bi-ayyi ālā'i Rabbi-kumā tukadhdhibān,* the *jinn* would respond with the words, "*Lā bi shai'in min ni'matī Rabbi-nā nukadhdhib,*" ('We do not deny any of our Lord's blessings.')
This tradition and some others indicate that *Sūrah Ar-Raḥmān* was revealed in early Makkan period.

Theme and Subject Matter: This is one of the most poetic and inspiring *Sūrah* of the Qur'ān. It repeats the refrain: *"Then which of the favors of your Lord will you deny?"* thirty-one times. This is the only *Sūrah* in the Qur'ān in which the *jinn* are directly addressed with humans; and both humans and *jinn* are made to realize the wonders of Allāh's Power, His countless blessings, and their own helplessness and accountability before Him. They are warned of the evil consequences of their disobedience to Allāh ﷻ and given glad tidings of the reward for obedience to Him.

ARABIC TEXT

بِسۡمِ ٱللَّهِ ٱلرَّحۡمَٰنِ ٱلرَّحِيمِ

ٱلرَّحۡمَٰنُ ﴿١﴾ عَلَّمَ ٱلۡقُرۡءَانَ ﴿٢﴾ خَلَقَ ٱلۡإِنسَٰنَ ﴿٣﴾
عَلَّمَهُ ٱلۡبَيَانَ ﴿٤﴾ ٱلشَّمۡسُ وَٱلۡقَمَرُ بِحُسۡبَانٖ ﴿٥﴾ وَٱلنَّجۡمُ
وَٱلشَّجَرُ يَسۡجُدَانِ ﴿٦﴾ وَٱلسَّمَآءَ رَفَعَهَا وَوَضَعَ ٱلۡمِيزَانَ
﴿٧﴾ أَلَّا تَطۡغَوۡاْ فِي ٱلۡمِيزَانِ ﴿٨﴾ وَأَقِيمُواْ ٱلۡوَزۡنَ بِٱلۡقِسۡطِ
وَلَا تُخۡسِرُواْ ٱلۡمِيزَانَ ﴿٩﴾ وَٱلۡأَرۡضَ وَضَعَهَا لِلۡأَنَامِ ﴿١٠﴾
فِيهَا فَٰكِهَةٞ وَٱلنَّخۡلُ ذَاتُ ٱلۡأَكۡمَامِ ﴿١١﴾ وَٱلۡحَبُّ ذُو ٱلۡعَصۡفِ
وَٱلرَّيۡحَانُ ﴿١٢﴾ فَبِأَيِّ ءَالَآءِ رَبِّكُمَا تُكَذِّبَانِ ﴿١٣﴾ خَلَقَ
ٱلۡإِنسَٰنَ مِن صَلۡصَٰلٖ كَٱلۡفَخَّارِ ﴿١٤﴾ وَخَلَقَ ٱلۡجَآنَّ
مِن مَّارِجٖ مِّن نَّارٖ ﴿١٥﴾ فَبِأَيِّ ءَالَآءِ رَبِّكُمَا تُكَذِّبَانِ ﴿١٦﴾
رَبُّ ٱلۡمَشۡرِقَيۡنِ وَرَبُّ ٱلۡمَغۡرِبَيۡنِ ﴿١٧﴾ فَبِأَيِّ ءَالَآءِ رَبِّكُمَا تُكَذِّبَانِ ﴿١٨﴾
مَرَجَ ٱلۡبَحۡرَيۡنِ يَلۡتَقِيَانِ ﴿١٩﴾ بَيۡنَهُمَا بَرۡزَخٞ لَّا يَبۡغِيَانِ ﴿٢٠﴾ فَبِأَيِّ ءَالَآءِ
رَبِّكُمَا تُكَذِّبَانِ ﴿٢١﴾ يَخۡرُجُ مِنۡهُمَا ٱللُّؤۡلُؤُ وَٱلۡمَرۡجَانُ ﴿٢٢﴾ فَبِأَيِّ
ءَالَآءِ رَبِّكُمَا تُكَذِّبَانِ ﴿٢٣﴾ وَلَهُ ٱلۡجَوَارِ ٱلۡمُنشَـَٔاتُ فِي ٱلۡبَحۡرِ كَٱلۡأَعۡلَٰمِ
﴿٢٤﴾ فَبِأَيِّ ءَالَآءِ رَبِّكُمَا تُكَذِّبَانِ ﴿٢٥﴾

TRANSLATIONS

1. (Allāh) Most Gracious {*Ar-Raḥmān*}
2. It is He Who has taught the Qur'ān.
3. He has created human {*al-Insān*):
4. He has taught him speech (and Intelligence) {*al-Bayān*}
5. The sun and the moon follow courses (exactly) computed;
6. And the herbs and the trees-both (alike) bow in adoration.
7. And the Firmament has He raised high, and He has set up the balance (of Justice) {*al-Mizān*},
8. In order that you may not transgress (due) balance.
9. So establish weight with justice and fall not short in the balance.
10. It is He Who has spread out the earth for (His) creatures:
11. Therein is fruit and date palms, producing spathes (enclosing dates):
12. Also corn, with (its) leaves and stalk for fodder, and sweet-smelling plants.
13. Then which of the favors {*ālā'i*} of your Lord will you deny?
14. He created human from sounding clay {*Ṣalṣāl*} like unto pottery {*Fakhkhār*},
15. And He created Jinns from fire free of smoke:
16. Then which of the favors of your Lord will you deny?
17. (He is) Lord of the two Easts and Lord of the two Wests:
18. Then which of the favors of your Lord

1. The Beneficent
2. Has made known the Qur'ān.
3. He has created man,
4. He has taught him utterance.
5. The sun and the moon are made punctual.
6. The stars and the trees adore.
7. And the sky He has uplifted; and He has set the measure,
8. That you exceed not the measure,
9. But observe the measure strictly, nor fall short thereof.
10. And the earth has He appointed for (His) creatures,
11. Wherein are fruit and sheathed palm trees,
12. Husked grain and scented herbs.
13. Which is it, of the favors of your Lord, that you deny?
14. He created man of clay like the potter's,
15. And the Jinn did He create of smokeless fire.
16. Which is it, of the favors of your Lord, that you deny?
17. Lord, of the two Easts, and Lord of the two Wests!
18. Which is it, of the favors of your Lord,

will you deny?

19. He has let free the two bodies of flowing water, meeting together:

20. Between them is a Barrier which they do not transgress:

21. Then which of the favors of your Lord will you deny?

22. Out of them come Pearls and Coral:

23. Then which of the favors of your Lord will you deny?

24. And His are the Ships sailing smoothly through the seas, lofty as mountains:

25. Then which of the favors of your Lord will you deny?

(A. Y. Ali)

that you deny?

19. He has loosed the two seas. They meet.

20. There is a barrier between them. They encroach not (one upon the other).

21. Which is it, of the favors of your Lord, that you deny?

22. There comes forth from both of them the pearl and coral stone.

23. Which is it, of the favors of your Lord, that you deny?

24. His are the ships displayed upon the sea, like banners.

25. Which is it, of the favors of your Lord, that you deny?

(M. M. Pickthal)

EXPLANATION (A. Y. Ali)

1: {*Ar-Raḥmān*, Most-Gracious, is one of the prominent names of Allāh سبحانه وتعالى. It is one of the three most repeated names in the Qur'ān, the other two being Allāh and *Ar-Raḥīm* (Most-Merciful). The entire *Sūrah* deals with counting the *Raḥmah* (Grace and Mercy) of Allāh سبحانه وتعالى to His creation, especially to human beings. (See also *Al-Fātiḥah* 1:2) AG}.

2: The Revelation comes from Allāh سبحانه وتعالى, Most Gracious, and it is one of the greatest Signs of His Grace and Favor. He is the source of all Light, and His Light is diffused throughout the universe.

3: {He has created human beings in the best mold. He has endowed them with intelligence to discover and a will to choose right from wrong. AG}.

4: *al-Bayān*: intelligent speech, power of expression, capacity to understand clearly the relationship between various things and to explain them. Allāh ﷻ has given this power exclusively to human beings. Besides this final revelation, the Qur'ān, He has aided us with revelation in nature and revelation through the earlier messengers.

5: In astronomy, there are exact mathematical laws that bear witness to Allāh's Wisdom and His Favors to His creatures. We all profit from heat and light, the four seasons, and the numerous changes in the tides and the atmosphere, upon which the constitution of our universe and the maintenance of all life depend.

6: *An-Najm*: may mean stars collectively, or herbs collectively. Perhaps, both meanings are implied. {All nature obeys and submits to the commands of Allāh ﷻ. AG}. All of nature adores Allāh ﷻ and submits to His orders. This is a recurring theme in the Qur'ān. (See *Al-Ḥajj* 22:18, *Ar-Ra'd* 13:15, and *An-Naḥl* 16: 48-49.)

7: *Al-Mīzān* or "the balance of justice" in this verse is connected with "the Balance" in the next two verses. The message here is that humans should act justly towards one another and observe due balance in all their actions, so that they follow the middle path and not cross any bounds.

The balance is also connected figuratively with the fact that:

(1) justice is a heavenly virtue
(2) the Heavens themselves are sustained by a mathematical balance

8: {In the same way that balance (*al-Mīzān*) is essential for maintaining cosmic order, it is also essential for maintaining order in our lives on earth. Proper balance in our business affairs and in our social lives is crucial for a just and peaceful society. AG}

9: The Qur'an clearly teaches that a person should be honest and straightforward in everyday life. A businessman must measure and weigh honestly his merchandise that he sells to others. He should be just, and honest in all his dealings, not only with other people, but with himself. He should also be sincere and honest in following Allāh's Law. We must keep the human world balanced, just as the heavenly world is kept balanced by Divine mathematical order.

10-12: How can Allāh's favors be counted? Look at the earth itself. Life and the conditions here are mutually balanced for Allāh's creatures. The Plant Kingdom produces a variety of fruits and grains for humans to enjoy. The grain harvest yields food for humans and fodder for animals. Plants provide food, sweet-smelling herbs, and flowers.

13: Both the pronoun "your" and the verb "will you deny" are used here in Arabic dual number. This whole *Sūrah* deals with duality, which leads to unity. All creation occurs in pairs (See notes *A<u>dh</u>-<u>dh</u>āriyāt* 51:49 and *Ṣabā* 34:36). The concepts mentioned in this *Sūrah* are described in pairs. Then there are human beings and *jinn*, two creations of Allāh ﷻ (see v. 15 note below). "Will you deny?" that is, fail to acknowledge the favors of Allāh ﷻ either in word, thought, or in conduct. If one misuses Allāh's gifts or ignores them, that is equivalent to ingratitude and refusal to profit by Allāh's infinite Mercy.

14: The creation of human beings and *jinn* is contrasted. *Al-Insān*, mankind, was made of sounding clay; dry and brittle, like pottery. *Jinn* (see next note) were made from a clear flame of fire. Each separate creation has capacities and possibilities bestowed upon it through Allāh's Grace alone. How can they deny Allāh's favors? (See also note to *Al-Ḥijr* 5:26).

15: The *jinn* are spirits, subtle like the flame of a fire. Being free from smoke implies that they are free from grossness. (See also *Al-An'ām* 6: 100 note for a more detailed discussion on *jinn*).

16: The refrain: "Which of the favors of the Lord will you deny?" appears thirty-one times in this *Sūrah*. Part of the idea of this refrain will be found in *An-Naḥl* 16:71-72, *<u>Gh</u>āfir* 40:81, and *An-Najm* 53:55.

17-18: The two Easts are the two extreme points at which the sun rises during the year, and includes all the points in between. Similarly, the two Wests include the two extreme points of the sun's setting, and all points in between. The dual number fits with the general atmosphere of duality in this *Sūrah*.

19: Allāh ﷻ is Lord of every region of the earth and sky, and He scatters His two seas {*Baḥrain*} or two bodies of flowing water (*Baḥr* is applied both to the salty sea and to freshwater). In the world, there are two bodies of water: (1) the great salt ocean, and (2) the bodies of sweet water (rivers, lakes or underground springs). Rain, as their source, makes them one; and their ultimate drainage into the ocean also makes them one. They are free to mingle and, in a sense, they do mingle.

20: There is also a regular water cycle: rivers flow to the sea and tidal rivers get sea-water for several miles up their estuaries at high tide. In spite of all this, the laws of gravitation are like a barrier or partition set by Allāh ﷻ, by which the two bodies of water are kept separate and distinct. In the case of rivers, such as the Mississippi or the Yangtse-Kiang, carrying large quantities of water to the sea, the river-water with its silt remains distinct from sea-water for a long distance out at sea. But the wonderful Sign is that the two bodies of water, though they pass through each other, remain distinctly separate, each with its own unique function.

21: Incidentally, this verse points to a fact which has only recently been discovered by science. This fact relates to the oceans of the world: they meet, and yet, each remains separate. For, Allāh ﷻ has placed "a barrier, a partition" between them.

22-23: Pearls are produced by the oyster and coral is produced by the polyp, a minute marine creature that works with millions of other creatures to produce reefs and islands on both sides of the Red Sea and in other parts of the world. Both pearls and coral are considered semi-precious, and are generally understood to mean gems in this context.

24-25: The ships, steamers; and by extension of analogy, airplanes and spaceships; are made by humans with the intelligence given to them by their Creator.

IMPORTANT POINTS TO LEARN AND REFLECT UPON

- The Merciful Lord (*Ar-Raḥmān*), in His kindness, taught us the meaning of the Qur'ān and taught us how to speak (*al-Bayān*).
- He has created a balanced universe; similarly, we should observe balance in our lives and dealings.
- He is the Lord Who Owns all the directions, and His favors are undeniable.

GLOSSARY WORDS

'Ālā'i, *al-Bayān*, *al-Mīzān*, *Ar-Raḥmān,* estuaries, grossness, mingle

VOCABULARY

سورة الرَّحْمٰن - ٥٥

الركوع ١ - Section 1

بِسْمِ ٱللَّهِ ٱلرَّحْمٰنِ ٱلرَّحِيمِ

(١) اَلرَّحْمٰنُ	The Most Gracious	(٨) اَلاَّ تَطْغَوْا	that you may not transgress
(٢) عَلَّمَ الْقُرْاٰنَ	He, Who taught the Qur'an	فِى الْمِيزَانِ	in the balance
(٣) خَلَقَ	He has created	(٩) وَ أَقِيمُوا	And establish
اَلْإِنْسَانَ	man	اَلْوَزْنَ	weight
(٤) عَلَّمَهُ الْبَيَانَ	He has taught him speech	بِالْقِسْطِ	with justice
(٥) اَلشَّمْسُ	The sun	وَ لَا تُخْسِرُوا	and fall not short
وَ الْقَمَرُ	and the moon	اَلْمِيزَانَ	in the balance
بِحُسْبَانٍ	follow courses (exactly)	(١٠) وَ الْأَرْضَ	And the earth
(٦) وَّ النَّجْمُ	And the herbs (or the stars)	وَضَعَهَا	He has spread out
وَ الشَّجَرُ	And the trees	لِلْأَنَامِ	for creatures
يَسْجُدَانِ	bow in adoration	(١١) فِيهَا فَاكِهَةٌ	Therein is fruit
(٧) وَ السَّمَآءَ	And the Heaven	وَّ النَّخْلُ	and date palms
رَفَعَهَا	He raised high	ذَاتُ الْأَكْمَامِ	producing spathes
وَوَضَعَ	and He has set up	(١٢) وَ الْحَبُّ	Also corn
اَلْمِيزَانَ	the Balance (of Justice)	و الْعَصْفِ	with leaves and stalk for fodder

وَ الرَّيْحَانُ	and sweet-smelling plants
(١٣) فَبِأَيِّ	Then which of
اٰ لَاءِ	the favors
رَبِّكُمَا	of your Lord
تُكَذِّبٰنِ	will you deny
(١٤) خَلَقَ الْإِنْسَانَ	He created humans
مِنْ صَلْصَالٍ	from sounding clay
كَالْفَخَّارِ	like unto pottery
(١٥) وَخَلَقَ	And He created
الجَآنَّ	Jinns
مِنْ مَّارِجٍ	of smoke
مِّن نَّارٍ	from fire free
(١٦) فَبِأَيِّ اٰ لَاءِ	Then which of the favors
رَبِّكُمَا	of your Lord
تُكَذِّبٰنِ	will you deny
(١٧) رَبُّ الْمَشْرِقَيْنِ	Lord of the two Easts
وَرَبُّ الْمَغْرِبَيْنِ	and Lord of the two Wests
(١٨) فَبِأَيِّ اٰ لَاءِ	Then which of the favors
رَبِّكُمَا	of your Lord
تُكَذِّبٰنِ	will you deny
(١٩) مَرَجَ	Of flowing

اَلْبَحْرَيْنِ	the two bodies of water
يَلْتَقِيٰنِ	meeting together
(٢٠) بَيْنَهُمَا	between them
بَرْزَخٌ	is a barrier
لَّا يَبْغِيٰنِ	which they do not cross
(٢١) فَبِأَيِّ اٰ لَاءِ	Then which of the favors
رَبِّكُمَا	of your Lord
تُكَذِّبٰنِ	will you deny
(٢٢) يَخْرُجُ مِنْهُمَا	Out of them come
اَللُّؤْلُؤُ	the pearls
وَ الْمَرْجَانُ	and the coral
(٢٣) فَبِأَيِّ اٰ لَاءِ	Then which of the favors
رَبِّكُمَا	of your Lord
تُكَذِّبٰنِ	will you deny
(٢٤) وَ لَهُ	And His are
اَلْجَوَارِ	the ships
اَلْمُنْشَئٰتُ	sailing smoothly
فِى الْبَحْرِ	through the sea
كَالْأَعْلَامِ	lofty as mountains
(٢٥) فَبِأَيِّ اٰ لَاءِ	Then which of the favors
رَبِّكُمَا تُكَذِّبٰنِ	of your Lord will you deny

Section 2: 26-45

SŪRAH AR-RAḤMĀN 55

The Most Gracious / The Beneficent

ARABIC TEXT

بِسْمِ ٱللَّهِ ٱلرَّحْمَٰنِ ٱلرَّحِيمِ

كُلُّ مَنْ عَلَيْهَا فَانٍ ﴿٢٦﴾ وَيَبْقَىٰ
وَجْهُ رَبِّكَ ذُو ٱلْجَلَٰلِ وَٱلْإِكْرَامِ ﴿٢٧﴾ فَبِأَىِّ ءَالَآءِ رَبِّكُمَا تُكَذِّبَانِ
﴿٢٨﴾ يَسْـَٔلُهُۥ مَن فِى ٱلسَّمَٰوَٰتِ وَٱلْأَرْضِ ۚ كُلَّ يَوْمٍ هُوَ فِى شَأْنٍ ﴿٢٩﴾ فَبِأَىِّ
ءَالَآءِ رَبِّكُمَا تُكَذِّبَانِ ﴿٣٠﴾ سَنَفْرُغُ لَكُمْ أَيُّهَ ٱلثَّقَلَانِ ﴿٣١﴾ فَبِأَىِّ
ءَالَآءِ رَبِّكُمَا تُكَذِّبَانِ ﴿٣٢﴾ يَٰمَعْشَرَ ٱلْجِنِّ وَٱلْإِنسِ إِنِ ٱسْتَطَعْتُمْ
أَن تَنفُذُوا۟ مِنْ أَقْطَارِ ٱلسَّمَٰوَٰتِ وَٱلْأَرْضِ فَٱنفُذُوا۟ ۚ لَا تَنفُذُونَ
إِلَّا بِسُلْطَٰنٍ ﴿٣٣﴾ فَبِأَىِّ ءَالَآءِ رَبِّكُمَا تُكَذِّبَانِ ﴿٣٤﴾ يُرْسَلُ عَلَيْكُمَا
شُوَاظٌ مِّن نَّارٍ وَنُحَاسٌ فَلَا تَنتَصِرَانِ ﴿٣٥﴾ فَبِأَىِّ ءَالَآءِ رَبِّكُمَا
تُكَذِّبَانِ ﴿٣٦﴾ فَإِذَا ٱنشَقَّتِ ٱلسَّمَآءُ فَكَانَتْ وَرْدَةً كَٱلدِّهَانِ
﴿٣٧﴾ فَبِأَىِّ ءَالَآءِ رَبِّكُمَا تُكَذِّبَانِ ﴿٣٨﴾ فَيَوْمَئِذٍ لَّا يُسْـَٔلُ عَن ذَنۢبِهِۦٓ
إِنسٌ وَلَا جَآنٌّ ﴿٣٩﴾ فَبِأَىِّ ءَالَآءِ رَبِّكُمَا تُكَذِّبَانِ ﴿٤٠﴾

يُعْرَفُ ٱلْمُجْرِمُونَ بِسِيمَٰهُمْ فَيُؤْخَذُ بِٱلنَّوَٰصِى وَٱلْأَقْدَامِ ﴿٤١﴾ فَبِأَىِّ
ءَالَآءِ رَبِّكُمَا تُكَذِّبَانِ ﴿٤٢﴾ هَٰذِهِۦ جَهَنَّمُ ٱلَّتِى يُكَذِّبُ بِهَا ٱلْمُجْرِمُونَ
﴿٤٣﴾ يَطُوفُونَ بَيْنَهَا وَبَيْنَ حَمِيمٍ ءَانٍ ﴿٤٤﴾ فَبِأَىِّ ءَالَآءِ رَبِّكُمَا تُكَذِّبَانِ ﴿٤٥﴾

TRANSLATIONS

26. All that is on earth will perish:

26. Everyone that is thereon will pass away;

27. But will abide (forever) the Face of your Lord - full of Majesty, Bounty and Honor {*Dhu (a)l-Jalā li wa (a)l-Ikrām*}.

27. There remains but the countenance of your Lord of Might and Glory.

28. Then which of the favors of your Lord will you deny?

28. Which is it, of the favors of your Lord, that you deny?

29. Of Him seeks (its needs) every creature in the heavens and on earth: every day in (new) Splendor does He (shine)!

29. All that are in the heavens and the earth entreat Him. Every day He exercises (universal) power.

30. Then which of the favors of your Lord will you deny?

30. Which is it, of the favors of your Lord, that you deny?

31. Soon shall We settle your affairs, O both you worlds {*ath-Thaqalān*}!

31. We shall dispose of you, O you two dependents (man and Jinn).

32. Then which of the favors of your Lord will you deny?

32. Which is it, of the favors of your Lord, that you deny?

33. O you assembly of Jinns and men! if it be you can pass beyond the zones of the heavens and the earth, pass you! not without authority {*as-Sulṭān*} shall you be able to pass!

33. O company of Jinn and men, if you have power to penetrate (all) regions of the heavens and the earth, then penetrate (them)! You will never penetrate them but with (Our) sanction.

34. Then which of the favors of your Lord will you deny?

35. On you will be sent (O you evil ones twain!) a flame of fire (to burn) and a smoke (to choke): No defense will you have:

36. Then which of the favors of your Lord will you deny?

37. When the sky is rent asunder, and it becomes red like ointment:

38. Then which of the favors of your Lord will you deny?

39. On that day no question will be asked of human or Jinn as to his sin,

40. Then which of the favors of your Lord will you deny?

41. (For) the sinners will be known by their Marks: and they will be seized by their forelocks and their feet.

42. Then which of the favors of your Lord will you deny?

43. This is the Hell which the Sinners deny:

44. In its midst and in the midst of boiling hot water will they wander round!

45. Then which of the favors of your Lord will you deny?

(A. Y. Ali)

34. Which is it, of the favors of your Lord, that you deny?

35. There will be sent, against you both, heat of fire and flash of brass, and you will not escape.

36. Which is it, of the favors of your Lord, that you deny?

37. And when the heaven splits asunder and becomes rosy like red hide -

38. Which is it, of the favors of your Lord, that you deny?

39. On that day neither man nor Jinn will be questioned of his sin.

40. Which is it, of the favors of your Lord, that you deny?

41. The guilty will be known by their marks, and will be taken by the forelocks and the feet.

42. Which is it, of the favors of your Lord, that you deny?

43. This is Hell which the guilty deny.

44. They go circling round between it and fierce, boiling water.

45. Which is it, of the favors of your Lord, that you deny?

(M. M. Pickthal)

EXPLANATION (A. Y. Ali)

26-28: Even the most magnificent works of humans are only temporary. They will all pass away at their appointed time. The only One to endure forever is Allāh ﷾, *Dhu (a)l-Jalāli wa (a)l-Ikrām* (Full of Majesty, Bounty and Honor). {Then Allāh ﷾ will order everything to be re-created and it will reappear. AG}.

Ikrām: two ideas are prominent in this word: (1) the idea of generosity, and (2) the idea of honor. Both these ideas are summed up in the term 'nobility.' To make the meaning clear in the translation, I have employed the two words, "Bounty and Honor" for the single word *Ikrām*.

29-30: Every single creature depends on Allāh ﷾ for its needs. *Shān* means state, splendor; momentous affair. Allāh's is the directing Hand in all affairs. His working shows new splendor every day, every hour, every moment.

31-32: *Ath-Thaqalān*: The two *thaqals* (weights) are *jinn* and human beings, who are burdened with responsibility or, as some commentators hold, with sin. Allāh ﷾ gives both the good and evil among the humans and *jinn* a chance in this life. However, this period will soon be over, and judgement will be established. To be given this warning is a favor from Allāh ﷾, for which we should be grateful.

33-34: O Humans and *Jinn,* do not be deceived into thinking that, because you do things in secret, or because some of your actions seem inconsequential right now, that you are saved. Judgement will soon come. You cannot possibly escape from the zones of which your lives have been cast, without authority from Allāh ﷾. All that has been promised to you will surely happen. (See also *Al-An'ām* 6:130-134, where *jinn* and humans are addressed collectively).

Note how gradually we have been led to the argument. 'The Signs of Allāh ﷾ are all around you, in revelation, in your intelligence, and in the nature which surrounds you.' All these things should teach you the Truth and warn you about the Future, which is more specifically referred to in the remainder of the *Sūrah*.

35-36: We now come to the terrors of the Day of Judgement for the disbelievers. Here, and in some of the verses that follow, (verses 40, 42 and 45 below), the refrain is attached with irony; almost as if it were being said: 'You used to laugh at the Revelation and at the warnings. Is not all that was said to you coming true?'

37-38: The sky will melt away like grease. The red color will be due to the flames and the heat. The whole world, as we now know it, will dissolve.

39-42: They will still be called to account for their sins, of course. The meaning here is that their personal responsibility will be enforced. Their own tongues and hands and feet will bear witness against them (*Ibrāhīm* 14:24). Everyone will bear marks on his person, showing his classification in the Final Account (See *Al-A'rāf* 7:48).

To give every chance to the accused, his record will be produced and shown to him (*Al-Ḥāqqa* 69:19, 25; *Al-Furqān* 18:49), and he will be given a chance to plead his case (*Al-A'rāf* 7: 53).

43-45: It will then become too real to the disbelievers, a reality they long denied. They will have no rest. The fire will burn, but not consume, them; and their drink will be boiling water.

IMPORTANT POINTS TO LEARN AND REFLECT UPON

- Only Allāh ﷻ is Eternal; everything He created will one day perish.
- No humans or jinn can escape Allāh's cosmic order, except through His permission.
- On the Day of Judgement, the sinners will be seized harshly, and will be known by special marks on their bodies.

GLOSSARY WORDS

disgrace, faculties, righteous, *as-Sulṭān, Thaqalān, Dhu (a)l Jalāli wa (a)l-Ikrām*

VOCABULARY

الركوع ٢ - Section 2

بِسْمِ ٱللَّهِ ٱلرَّحْمَٰنِ ٱلرَّحِيمِ

(٢٦) كُلُّ مَنْ	All that is
عَلَيْهَا	on it (earth)
فَانٍ	will perish
(٢٧) وَ يَبْقَىٰ	But will abide
وَجْهُ	His Face
رَبِّكَ	of your Lord
ذُو الْجَلَٰلِ	Full of Majesty
وَ الْإِكْرَامِ	and Bounty and Honor
(٢٨) فَبِأَيِّ ءَالَآءِ	Then which of the favours
رَبِّكُمَا	of your Lord
تُكَذِّبَانِ	will you deny
(٢٩) يَسْئَلُهُ	Of Him seeks
مَنْ فِى السَّمَٰوَٰتِ	in the heavens
وَ الْأَرْضِ	and on earth
كُلَّ يَوْمٍ	every day
هُوَ فِى شَأْنٍ	in splendor He shines
(٣٠) فَبِأَيِّ ءَالَآءِ	Then which of the favors
رَبِّكُمَا	of your Lord
تُكَذِّبَانِ	will you deny
(٣١) سَنَفْرُغُ لَكُمْ	We shall settle your affair
أَيُّهَ	O both
الثَّقَلَانِ	you worlds (dependents)
(٣٢) فَبِأَيِّ ءَالَآءِ	Then which of the favors
رَبِّكُمَا	of your Lord
تُكَذِّبَانِ	will you deny
(٣٣) يَٰمَعْشَرَ	O you assembly
الْجِنِّ	of Jinns
وَ الْإِنْسِ	and humans
إِنِ اسْتَطَعْتُمْ	If it be you
أَنْ تَنْفُذُوا	can pass beyond
مِنْ أَقْطَارِ	the zones
السَّمَٰوَٰتِ	of the heavens
وَ الْأَرْضِ	and the earth
فَانْفُذُوا	then pass you
لَا تَنْفُذُونَ	you shall not be able to pass
إِلَّا بِسُلْطَٰنٍ	but with the Authority

(٣٤) فَبِأَيِّ آلَاءِ	Then which of the favors	(٣٩) فَيَوْمَئِذٍ	On the Day
رَبِّكُمَا	of your Lord	لَّا يُسْئَلُ	no question are asked
تُكَذِّبَانِ	will you deny	عَنْ ذَنْبِهِ	as to his sin
(٣٥) يُرْسَلُ عَلَيْكُمَا	On you will be sent	إِنْسٌ	of human
شُوَاظٌ	a flame	وَّلَا جَانٌّ	or Jinn
مِّن نَّارٍ	of fire	(٤٠) فَبِأَيِّ آلَاءِ	Then which of the favors
وَنُحَاسٌ	and a (flash of) molten	رَبِّكُمَا	of your Lord
فَلَا تَنْتَصِرَانِ	no defence will you have	تُكَذِّبَانِ	will you deny
(٣٦) فَبِأَيِّ آلَاءِ	Then which of the favors	(٤١) يُعْرَفُ	Will be known
رَبِّكُمَا	of your Lord	الْمُجْرِمُونَ	the sinners
تُكَذِّبَانِ	will you deny	بِسِيمَاهُمْ	by their marks
(٣٧) فَإِذَا	When	يُؤْخَذُ	and they will be seized
انْشَقَّتِ	is split asunder	بِالنَّوَاصِي	by their forelocks
السَّمَاءُ	the sky	وَالْأَقْدَامِ	and their feet
فَكَانَتْ	and it becomes	(٤٢) فَبِأَيِّ آلَاءِ	Then which of the favors
وَرْدَةً	red	رَبِّكُمَا	of your Lord
كَالدِّهَانِ	like ointment	تُكَذِّبَانِ	will you deny
(٣٨) فَبِأَيِّ آلَاءِ	Then which of the favours	(٤٣) هَٰذِهِ جَهَنَّمُ	This is Hell
رَبِّكُمَا	of your Lord	الَّتِي يُكَذِّبُ بِهَا	that which deny it
تُكَذِّبَانِ	will you deny	الْمُجْرِمُونَ	the sinners

يَطُوفُونَ (٤٤)	Will they wander	اٰنٍ	water
بَيْنَهَا	around it	(٤٥) فَبِأَىِّ اٰ لَآءِ	Then which of the favors
وَبَيْنَ	and in the midst	رَبِّكُمَا	of your Lord
حَمِيمٍ	of boiling water	تُكَذِّبٰنِ	will you deny

Section 3: 46-78

SŪRAH AR-RAḤMĀN 55

The Most Gracious / The Beneficent

ARABIC TEXT

بِسْمِ ٱللَّهِ ٱلرَّحْمَٰنِ ٱلرَّحِيمِ

وَلِمَنْ خَافَ مَقَامَ رَبِّهِۦ جَنَّتَانِ ﴿٤٦﴾ فَبِأَيِّ ءَالَآءِ رَبِّكُمَا تُكَذِّبَانِ

﴿٤٧﴾ ذَوَاتَآ أَفْنَانٍ ﴿٤٨﴾ فَبِأَيِّ ءَالَآءِ رَبِّكُمَا تُكَذِّبَانِ ﴿٤٩﴾ فِيهِمَا عَيْنَانِ

تَجْرِيَانِ ﴿٥٠﴾ فَبِأَيِّ ءَالَآءِ رَبِّكُمَا تُكَذِّبَانِ ﴿٥١﴾ فِيهِمَا مِن كُلِّ فَٰكِهَةٍ

زَوْجَانِ ﴿٥٢﴾ فَبِأَيِّ ءَالَآءِ رَبِّكُمَا تُكَذِّبَانِ ﴿٥٣﴾ مُتَّكِـِٔينَ عَلَىٰ فُرُشٍۭ

بَطَآئِنُهَا مِنْ إِسْتَبْرَقٍ ۚ وَجَنَى ٱلْجَنَّتَيْنِ دَانٍ ﴿٥٤﴾ فَبِأَيِّ ءَالَآءِ رَبِّكُمَا

تُكَذِّبَانِ ﴿٥٥﴾ فِيهِنَّ قَٰصِرَٰتُ ٱلطَّرْفِ لَمْ يَطْمِثْهُنَّ إِنسٌ قَبْلَهُمْ

وَلَا جَآنٌّ ﴿٥٦﴾ فَبِأَيِّ ءَالَآءِ رَبِّكُمَا تُكَذِّبَانِ ﴿٥٧﴾ كَأَنَّهُنَّ ٱلْيَاقُوتُ

وَٱلْمَرْجَانُ ﴿٥٨﴾ فَبِأَيِّ ءَالَآءِ رَبِّكُمَا تُكَذِّبَانِ ﴿٥٩﴾ هَلْ جَزَآءُ

ٱلْإِحْسَٰنِ إِلَّا ٱلْإِحْسَٰنُ ﴿٦٠﴾ فَبِأَيِّ ءَالَآءِ رَبِّكُمَا تُكَذِّبَانِ

﴿٦١﴾ وَمِن دُونِهِمَا جَنَّتَانِ ﴿٦٢﴾ فَبِأَيِّ ءَالَآءِ رَبِّكُمَا تُكَذِّبَانِ

﴿٦٣﴾ مُدْهَآمَّتَانِ ﴿٦٤﴾ فَبِأَيِّ ءَالَآءِ رَبِّكُمَا تُكَذِّبَانِ ﴿٦٥﴾ فِيهِمَا

عَيْنَانِ نَضَّاخَتَانِ ﴿٦٦﴾ فَبِأَيِّ ءَالَآءِ رَبِّكُمَا تُكَذِّبَانِ ﴿٦٧﴾

فِيهِمَا فَٰكِهَةٌ وَنَخْلٌ وَرُمَّانٌ ٦٨ فَبِأَيِّ ءَالَآءِ رَبِّكُمَا تُكَذِّبَانِ ٦٩

فِيهِنَّ خَيْرَٰتٌ حِسَانٌ ٧٠ فَبِأَيِّ ءَالَآءِ رَبِّكُمَا تُكَذِّبَانِ ٧١ حُورٌ

مَّقْصُورَٰتٌ فِى ٱلْخِيَامِ ٧٢ فَبِأَيِّ ءَالَآءِ رَبِّكُمَا تُكَذِّبَانِ ٧٣

لَمْ يَطْمِثْهُنَّ إِنسٌ قَبْلَهُمْ وَلَا جَآنٌّ ٧٤ فَبِأَيِّ ءَالَآءِ رَبِّكُمَا تُكَذِّبَانِ

٧٥ مُتَّكِـِٔينَ عَلَىٰ رَفْرَفٍ خُضْرٍ وَعَبْقَرِىٍّ حِسَانٍ ٧٦ فَبِأَيِّ

ءَالَآءِ رَبِّكُمَا تُكَذِّبَانِ ٧٧ تَبَٰرَكَ ٱسْمُ رَبِّكَ ذِى ٱلْجَلَٰلِ وَٱلْإِكْرَامِ ٧٨

TRANSLATIONS

46. But for such as fear the time when they will stand before (the Judgement Seat of) their Lord, there will be two Gardens {*Jannatān*}-

47. Then which of the favors of your Lord will you deny?

48. Containing all kinds (of trees and delights)-

49. Then which of the favors of your Lord will you deny?

50. In them (each) will be two Springs flowing (free);

51. Then which of the favors of your Lord will you deny?

52. In them will be Fruits of every kind,

46. But for him who fears the standing before his Lord there are two gardens.

47. Which is it, of the favors of your Lord, that you deny?

48. Of spreading branches

49. Which is it, of the favors of your Lord, that you deny?

50. Wherein are two fountains flowing.

51. Which is it, of the favors of your Lord, that you deny?

52. Wherein is every kind of fruit in pairs.

two and two.

53. Then which of the favors of your Lord will you deny?

54. They will recline on Carpets, whose inner linings will be of rich brocade: the Fruit of the Gardens will be Near (and easy of reach).

55. Then which of the favors of your Lord will you deny?

56. In them will be (Maidens), Chaste, restraining their glances, whom no human or Jinn before them has touched -

57. Then which of the favors of your Lord will you deny?

58. Like unto rubies and coral.

59. Then which of the favors of your Lord will you deny?

60. Is there any Reward for Good - other than Good?

61. Then which of the favors of your Lord will you deny?

62. And besides these two, there are two other Gardens -

63. Then which of the favors of your Lord will you deny?

64. Dark green in color (from plentiful watering).

65. Then which of the favors of your Lord will you deny?

66. In them (each) will be two springs pouring forth water in continuous

53. Which is it, of the favors of your Lord, that you deny?

54. Reclining upon couches lined with silk brocade, the fruit of both gardens near to hand.

55. Which is it, of the favors of your Lord, that you deny?

56. Therein are those of modest gaze, whom neither man nor Jinn will have touched before them.

57. Which is it, of the favors of your Lord, that you deny?

58. (In beauty) like the jacinth and the coral stone.

59. Which is it, of the favors of your Lord, that you deny?

60. Is the reward of goodness aught save goodness?

61. Which is it, of the favors of your Lord, that you deny?

62. And beside them are two other gardens,

63. Which is it, of the favors of your Lord, that you deny?

64. Dark green with foliage.

65. Which is it, of the favors of your Lord, that you deny?

66. Wherein are two abundant springs.

abundance:

67. Then which of the favors of your Lord will you deny?

68. In them will be Fruits, and dates and pomegranates:

69. Then which of the favors of your Lord will you deny?

70. In them will be fair (Companions), good, beautiful -

71. Then which of the favors of your Lord will you deny?

72. Companions restrained (as to their glances), in (goodly) pavilions -

73. Then which of the favor of your Lord will you deny?

74. Whom no human or Jinn before them has touched -

75. Then which of the favors of your Lord will you deny?

76. Reclining on green Cushions and rich Carpets of beauty.

77. Then which of the favors of your Lord will you deny?

78. Blessed be the name of your Lord, full of Majesty, Bounty and Honor.

(A. Y. Ali)

67. Which is it, of the favors of your Lord, that you deny?

68. Wherein is fruit, the date palm and pomegranate

69. Which is it, of the favors of your Lord, that you deny?

70. Wherein (are found) the good and beautiful

71. Which is it, of the favors of your Lord, that you deny?-

72. Fair ones, closely guarded in pavilions

73. Which is it, of the favors of your Lord, that you deny?

74. Whom neither man nor Jinn will have touched before them -

75. Which is it, of the favors of your Lord, that you deny? -

76. Reclining on green cushions and fair carpets.

77. Which is it, of the favors of your Lord, that you deny?

78. Blessed be the name of your Lord, Mighty and Glorious!

(M. M. Pickthal)

EXPLANATION (A. Y. Ali, revised)

46-49: We now come to a description of the state of the Blessed. Here, two more Gardens are mentioned. The Gardens total four in number, counting the two gardens mentioned in verses 62-76. Opinions are divided about this, but the best opinion is that the two gardens mentioned in verses 46-61 refer to the gardens nearest to Allāh ﷻ (*Muqarrabūn*), and those in verses 62-76 are for the Companions of the Right Hand. Why two for each? The duality is to express variety, and the whole theme of the *Sūrah* runs in twos. It reflects the idea that there will be no dullness or uniformity, and that there will be freshness in change: there will be Bliss upon Bliss.

50-53: The duality of springs (of water) and the duality of fruits represent the same theme of the duality as presented in the previous verse.

54-56: The toil and fatigue of this life will be over (See also *Al-Fāṭir* 35:35).

56-57: Here, as elsewhere in the Qur'ān, the Promised Companions have the excellent characteristics of purity, beauty, grace, innocence and goodwill. (See also notes to *Ad-Dukhān* 44:54; *Aṣ-Ṣāffāt* 37: 48)

58-59: Delicate pink refers to the complexions of the Promised Companions, and their beauty of form. The gems also indicate their worth and dignity.

60-61: This sums up all the descriptions of the rewards for goodness and piety {*'Iḥsān*}. But the fullest expression can only be given in abstract terms: "Is there any reward for good other than good?"

62-63: {"Another two gardens," as in verse 46, implies richness and diversity. There is no uniformity or dullness in *Jannah*. AG}.

64-65: "Dark-green in color": these gardens will also be fruitful and flourishing, and watered plentifully; but their characteristics will be different.

66-67: In comparison to the springs of the other two gardens, described in 55:50 above, these springs would seem to irrigate crops of vegetables and fruits requiring a constant supply of abundant water.

68-69: See note 55:52 above, where "fruits of every kind" is mentioned. The duality implies diversity, freshness and change.

70-71: See note 55:56 above. Goodness and Beauty are especially feminine attributes.

72-73: *Maqṣūrāt* here is the passive participle of the same verb, as the active participle *Qāṣirāt* in 55:56, *Aṣ-Ṣāffāt* 37:48 and *Ṣād* 38:52. By translating *Qāṣirāt* as "restraining (their glances)," it is appropriate to translate the passive *Maqṣūrāt* as "restrained (as to their glances)." This is the only place in the Qur'ān where the passive form occurs. The pavilions seem to add dignity to their status. In the other gardens (55:58), the description "like rubies and corals" is perhaps an indication of higher dignity.

74-75: Pure and innocent virgins will be their constant companions.

76-77: The parallel words for the other two gardens in 55: 54 above suggest perhaps a higher dignity. *Rafraf* is usually translated as 'Cushions' or 'Pillows,' and I have followed this meaning in view of the word 'reclining.' Another interpretation is 'Meadows,' in view of the adjective 'green'-*'abqarī*: carpets richly figured and dyed, and skillfully worked.

78: This minor echo completes the symmetry of the two leading ideas of this *Sūrah*: the Bounty and Majesty of Allāh ﷻ, and our duty to make ourselves worthy of being near to Allāh ﷻ.

IMPORTANT POINTS TO LEARN AND REFLECT UPON

- For the righteous and God-fearing, there will be gardens of delight, companionship of the pure ones, and pleasures that cannot be described in human words.
- Every good action done by humans is rewarded with good from Allāh ﷻ in the *'Ākhirah*.
- Then which of the favors of our Merciful Allāh ﷻ do we deny?

GLOSSARY WORDS

'abqarī, 'Iḥsān, Jannatān, Maqṣūrāt, Muqarrabūn, Rafraf

VOCABULARY

الركوع ٣ - Section 3

بِسْمِ ٱللَّهِ ٱلرَّحْمَٰنِ ٱلرَّحِيمِ

(٤٦) وَ لِمَنْ خَافَ	But for such who fears	(٥٢) فِيهِمَا	In them
مَقَامَ	the standing before	مِنْ كُلِّ	of every kind
رَبِّهِ	his Lord	فَاكِهَةٍ	fruits
جَنَّتَانِ	are two Gardens	زَوْجَانِ	two and two (pairs)
(٤٧) فَبِأَيِّ آلَاءِ	Then which of the favors	(٥٣) فَبِأَيِّ آلَاءِ	Then which of the favors
رَبِّكُمَا	of your Lord	رَبِّكُمَا تُكَذِّبَانِ	of your Lord will you deny
تُكَذِّبَانِ	will you deny	(٥٤) مُتَّكِئِينَ	They will recline
(٤٨) ذَوَاتَا أَفْنَانٍ	Abounding in branches	عَلَىٰ فُرُشٍ	on Carpets
(٤٩) فَبِأَيِّ آلَاءِ	Then which of the favors	بَطَائِنُهَا	inner linings
رَبِّكُمَا تُكَذِّبَانِ	of your Lord will you deny	مِنْ إِسْتَبْرَقٍ	of rich brocade
(٥٠) فِيهِمَا	In them	وَجَنَى	the fruit
عَيْنَانِ	two springs	الْجَنَّتَيْنِ	of the two Gardens
تَجْرِيَانِ	flowing	دَانٍ	will be near
(٥١) فَبِأَيِّ آلَاءِ	Then which of the favors	(٥٥) فَبِأَيِّ آلَاءِ	Then which of the favors
رَبِّكُمَا تُكَذِّبَانِ	of your Lord will you deny	رَبِّكُمَا تُكَذِّبَانِ	of your Lord will you deny

(٥٦) فِيهِنَّ	In them	(٦٣) فَبِأَىِّ ا لَاءِ	Then which of the favors
قٰصِرٰتُ	(maidens) chaste	رَبِّكُمَا تُكَذِّبٰنِ	of your Lord will you deny
الطَّرْفِ	restraining their glances	(٦٤) مُدْهَآمَّتٰنِ	Dark green in color
لَمْ يَطْمِثْهُنَّ	none has touched	(٦٥) فَبِأَىِّ ا لَاءِ	Then which of the favors
إِنْسٌ	human	رَبِّكُمَا تُكَذِّبٰنِ	of your Lord will you deny
قَبْلَهُمْ	before them	(٦٦) فِيهِمَا	In them
وَ لَا جَآنٌّ	and nor Jinn	عَيْنٰنِ	two springs
(٥٧) فَبِأَىِّ ا لَاءِ	Then which of the favors	نَضَّاخَتٰنِ	pouring forth water
رَبِّكُمَا تُكَذِّبٰنِ	of your Lord will you deny	(٦٧) فَبِأَىِّ ا لَاءِ	Then which of the favors
(٥٨) كَأَنَّهُنَّ	Like unto	رَبِّكُمَا تُكَذِّبٰنِ	of your Lord will you deny
الْيَاقُوتُ	the rubies	(٦٨) فِيهِمَا	In them
وَ الْمَرْجَانُ	and the coral	فَاكِهَةٌ	fruits
(٥٩) فَبِأَىِّ ا لَاءِ	Then which of the favors	وَّ نَخْلٌ	and dates
رَبِّكُمَا تُكَذِّبٰنِ	of your Lord will you deny	وَّ رُمَّانٌ	and pomegranates
(٦٠) هَلْ جَزَآءُ	Is there any Reward	(٦٩) فَبِأَىِّ ا لَاءِ	Then which of the favors
الْإِحْسَانِ	for good	رَبِّكُمَا تُكَذِّبٰنِ	of your Lord will you deny
إِلَّا الْإِحْسَانُ	other than good	(٧٠) فِيهِنَّ	In them
(٦١) فَبِأَىِّ ا لَاءِ	Then which of the favors	خَيْرٰتٌ	fair (companions)
رَبِّكُمَا تُكَذِّبٰنِ	of your Lord will you deny	حِسَانٌ	good, beautiful
(٦٢) وَمِنْ دُونِهِمَا	And besides these two	(٧١) فَبِأَىِّ ا لَاءِ	Then which of the favors
جَنَّتٰنِ	two other Gardens	رَبِّكُمَا تُكَذِّبٰنِ	of your Lord will you deny

(٧٢) حُورٌ	Companions, maidens	(٧٦) مُتَّكِـِٔينَ	Reclining
مَّقْصُورٰتٌ	restrained	عَلٰى رَفْرَفٍ خُضْرٍ	on green cushions
فِى الْخِيَامِ	in (goodly) pavilions	وَّعَبْقَرِىٍّ	and rich carpets
(٧٣) فَبِأَىِّ اٰلَآءِ	Then which of the favors	حِسَانٍ	(of) beauty
رَبِّكُمَا تُكَذِّبٰنِ	of your Lord will you deny	(٧٧) فَبِأَىِّ اٰلَآءِ	Then which of the favors
(٧٤) لَمْ يَطْمِثْهُنَّ	not touched	رَبِّكُمَا تُكَذِّبٰنِ	of your Lord will you deny
إِنْسٌ	by human	(٧٨) تَبٰرَكَ	Blessed
قَبْلَهُمْ	before them	اِسْمُ	(the) name (of)
وَ لَا جَآنٌّ	nor by Jinn	رَبِّكَ	your Lord
(٧٥) فَبِأَىِّ اٰلَآءِ	Then which of the favors	ذِى الْجَلٰلِ	full of Majesty, Bounty
رَبِّكُمَا تُكَذِّبٰنِ	of your Lord will you deny	وَ الْإِكْرَامِ	and Honor

Section 1:1-9

سُورَةُ الصَّفِّ

SŪRAH AṢ-ṢAFF 61: 1-14

The Battle Array / The Ranks

Name: The *Sūrah* derives its name from the word *Ṣaffan* (verse 4), meaning "standing in a row, joining ranks, and being disciplined in battle array. This implies unity and discipline.

Period of Revelation: The subject matter indicates that this *Sūrah* was revealed in the period soon after the Battle of Uḥud (3 AH).

Theme and Subject Matter: Its theme exhorts the Muslims to act according to their speech and be sincere and steadfast in their Faith, to join the ranks {*Ṣaffan*}, and to struggle {make *Jihād*} with their lives in the cause of Allāh سُبْحَانَهُ وَتَعَالَىٰ.

The Muslims are warned not to act as the Israelites did towards the Prophets Moses and Jesus عَلَيْهِمَا ٱلسَّلَامُ (peace be upon them).

The Believers are told that the way to success, both here and in the Hereafter, is through right beliefs and righteous actions.

ARABIC TEXT

بِسۡمِ ٱللَّهِ ٱلرَّحۡمَٰنِ ٱلرَّحِيمِ

سَبَّحَ لِلَّهِ مَا فِي ٱلسَّمَٰوَٰتِ وَمَا فِي ٱلۡأَرۡضِۖ وَهُوَ ٱلۡعَزِيزُ ٱلۡحَكِيمُ

١ يَٰٓأَيُّهَا ٱلَّذِينَ ءَامَنُواْ لِمَ تَقُولُونَ مَا لَا تَفۡعَلُونَ ٢

كَبُرَ مَقۡتًا عِندَ ٱللَّهِ أَن تَقُولُواْ مَا لَا تَفۡعَلُونَ ٣ إِنَّ

ٱللَّهَ يُحِبُّ ٱلَّذِينَ يُقَٰتِلُونَ فِي سَبِيلِهِۦ صَفًّا كَأَنَّهُم
بُنْيَٰنٌ مَّرْصُوصٌ ﴿٤﴾ وَإِذْ قَالَ مُوسَىٰ لِقَوْمِهِۦ يَٰقَوْمِ لِمَ
تُؤْذُونَنِي وَقَد تَّعْلَمُونَ أَنِّي رَسُولُ ٱللَّهِ إِلَيْكُمْ فَلَمَّا
زَاغُوٓا۟ أَزَاغَ ٱللَّهُ قُلُوبَهُمْ وَٱللَّهُ لَا يَهْدِي ٱلْقَوْمَ ٱلْفَٰسِقِينَ ﴿٥﴾
وَإِذْ قَالَ عِيسَى ٱبْنُ مَرْيَمَ يَٰبَنِيٓ إِسْرَٰٓءِيلَ إِنِّي رَسُولُ ٱللَّهِ إِلَيْكُم مُّصَدِّقًا
لِّمَا بَيْنَ يَدَيَّ مِنَ ٱلتَّوْرَىٰةِ وَمُبَشِّرًۢا بِرَسُولٍ يَأْتِي مِنۢ بَعْدِي ٱسْمُهُۥٓ أَحْمَدُ فَلَمَّا
جَآءَهُم بِٱلْبَيِّنَٰتِ قَالُوا۟ هَٰذَا سِحْرٌ مُّبِينٌ ﴿٦﴾ وَمَنْ أَظْلَمُ مِمَّنِ ٱفْتَرَىٰ
عَلَى ٱللَّهِ ٱلْكَذِبَ وَهُوَ يُدْعَىٰٓ إِلَى ٱلْإِسْلَٰمِ وَٱللَّهُ لَا يَهْدِي ٱلْقَوْمَ ٱلظَّٰلِمِينَ
﴿٧﴾ يُرِيدُونَ لِيُطْفِـُٔوا۟ نُورَ ٱللَّهِ بِأَفْوَٰهِهِمْ وَٱللَّهُ مُتِمُّ نُورِهِۦ وَلَوْ كَرِهَ
ٱلْكَٰفِرُونَ ﴿٨﴾ هُوَ ٱلَّذِيٓ أَرْسَلَ رَسُولَهُۥ بِٱلْهُدَىٰ وَدِينِ ٱلْحَقِّ لِيُظْهِرَهُۥ
عَلَى ٱلدِّينِ كُلِّهِۦ وَلَوْ كَرِهَ ٱلْمُشْرِكُونَ ﴿٩﴾

TRANSLATIONS

1. Whatever is in the heavens and on earth, let it declare the Praises and Glory of Allāh: for He is the Exalted in Might, the Wise.

2. O you who believe! Why say you that

1. All that is in the heavens and all that is in the earth glorifies Allāh, and He is the Mighty, the Wise.

2. O you who believe! why say you that

which you do not?

3. Grievously odious is it in the sight of Allāh that you say that which you do not.

4. Truly Allāh loves those who fight in His Cause in battle array {*Ṣaffan*}, as if they were a solid cemented structure {*Bunyānum Marṣūṣ*}.

5. And remember, Moses said to his people: "O my people! why do you vex and insult me, though you know that I am the messenger of Allāh (sent) to you?" Then when they went wrong, Allāh let their hearts go wrong. For Allāh guides not those who are rebellious transgressors.

6. And remember, Jesus, the son of Mary {'Īsa ibn Maryam}, said: "O Children of Israel! I am the messenger of Allāh (sent) to you, confirming the Law (which came) before me, and giving glad Tidings of a Messenger to come after me, whose name shall be Aḥmad." But when he came to them with Clear Signs, they said, "This is evident sorcery!"

7. Who does greater wrong than one who invents falsehood against Allāh, even as he is being invited to Islam? And Allah guides not those who do wrong.

8. Their intention is to extinguish Allāh's Light {*Nūr(u)Allāhi*} (by blowing) with their mouths: but Allāh will complete (the revelation of) His Light, even though the Unbelievers may detest (it).

9. It is He Who has sent His Messenger with Guidance and the Religion of Truth,

which you do not?

3. It is most hateful in the sight of Allāh that you say that which you do not.

4. Lo! Allāh loves those who battle for His cause in ranks, as if they were a solid structure.

5. And (remember) when Moses {Mūsa} said unto his people: O my people! Why persecute you me, when you well know that I am Allāh's messenger unto you? So when they went astray Allāh sent their hearts astray. And Allāh guides not the evil-living folk.

6. And when Jesus son of Mary {`Īsa ibn Maryam} said: O Children of Israel! Lo! I am the messenger of Allāh unto you, confirming that which was (revealed) before me in the Torah, and bringing good tidings of a messenger who comes after me, whose name is the Praised One. Yet when he has come unto them with clear proofs, they say: This is mere magic.

7. And who does greater wrong than he who invents a lie against Allāh when he is summoned unto Al-Islam. And Allāh guides not wrongdoing folk.

8. Fain would they put out the light of Allāh with their mouths, but Allāh will perfect His light, however much the disbelievers are averse.

9. He it is who has sent His messenger with the guidance and the religion of truth,

that he may proclaim it over all religion, even though the Pagans may detest (it).	that He may make it conqueror of all religion, however much idolaters may be averse.
(A. Y. Ali)	*(M. M. Pickthal)*

EXPLANATION (A. Y. Ali, revised)

1: This verse is identical to *Al-Ḥashr* 59:1. It illustrates the theme of Allāh's Power defeating the plans of His enemies. The emphasis here is our need for unshaken discipline if we are to receive the help of Allāh ﷻ.

2-3: At Uḥud, the Prophet's orders were disobeyed, and thus, discipline was broken. Before the Battle, people had spoken of unconditional obedience to the Prophet, but they failed to back up their words with firm action. When human deeds do not match their words, their conduct is absolutely despised in the sight of Allāh ﷻ. Only Allāh's Mercy can save them from disaster. (See also note *Āl-'Imrān* 3:121).

4: A striking example of order, discipline, and courage is a battle front in which a large number of people stand together against enemy attack, as if they were a solid wall. "A solid cemented structure" {*Bunyānum Marṣūṣ*} is even a better analogy than "solid wall." The "structure" or building symbolizes a diversified organization, unified and strong; each part contributing to the strength of the whole in its own way. (See also *Aṣ-Ṣāffāt* 37: 1 and note)

5: The people of Moses often rebelled against him and insulted him. They were not ignorant, but were selfish and rebellious, for which they received Divine punishment. The *'Ummah* of Islām should remember this and should avoid any deviation from the Law of Allāh ﷻ. When a sinner deviates from the right way, he closes the doors of Allāh's Mercy. There is still a chance for one to return. However, if one rebels repeatedly, Allāh ﷻ withdraws His protecting Grace, and the sinner's heart is tainted with a permanent disease that cannot be cured. The sinner's spiritual state is ruined.

6: The mission of Jesus 🕊 was limited to his own people, the Jews. (See *Matthew*10:5-6. See also *Matthew* 15:24: "I am not sent but to the lost sheep of Israel." See also *Matthew*15:26: "It is not meet to take the children's bread, and to cast it to dogs." {Jesus foretold the coming of the Prophet as a 'Comforter' for all humanity. (*Saba* 34:28) A.G.}

"Aḥmad" or "Muḥammad" (the Praised One), is almost a translation of the Greek word 'Pariclytos.' In the present Gospel of John (14:16, 15:26, and 16:7), the word 'Comforter' in the English version is the translation of the Greek word 'Paracletes,' meaning 'Advocate' or 'one called to the help of another; a kind friend.' Our scholars believe that Paracletes is a corrupt reading for Pariclytos and that in their original saying of Jesus 🕊, there was a prophecy of our Prophet Aḥmad ﷺ by name.

Even if we read Paraclete (translated as 'advocate' or 'friend'), it would apply to the Holy Prophet ﷺ more appropriately than to any other human being. He is "a Mercy for all creatures" (*Al-Anbiyā* 21:107) and "most kind and merciful to the Believers" (*At-Tawbah* 9:128). (See also note to 3:81).

The coming of our Prophet ﷺ was predicted in many ways. When he came, he brought forth many Clear Signs. His whole life was one vast miracle. He fought and won against all odds with Allāh's support.

7: It is wrong to uphold falsehoods and support superstitions, but it is especially wrong when humans oppose the light of Truth: Islām. Allāh's guidance is available for all to take advantage of, but He withdraws His Grace from those who do wrong.

8: Allāh's Light cannot be put out by ignorant disbelievers. "With their mouths" also implies the false rumors against the Truth of Islām. The more the foolish ones try to put out Allāh's Light, the clearer it shines to shame them!

9: "Over-all religion" is singular, and not plural ('over all other religions'). There is really only one true Religion. Following the Message of Allāh ﷻ and submitting completely to His Will is called Islām. It is the same religion that was preached by Abraham 🕊, Moses 🕊, Jesus 🕊 and all the other prophets. It was finally revealed to Prophet Muḥammad ﷺ, and Allāh ﷻ promises that the Truth of Islām will prevail over all.

IMPORTANT POINTS TO LEARN AND REFLECT UPON

- Most disliked in the Sight of Allāh ﷻ is that we say something we do not really mean.
- The coming of Rasūlullāh ﷺ was foretold by `Īsa ؑ and other messengers.
- Allāh ﷻ has sent His Messenger ﷺ with guidance and the true religion of Islam so that it will triumph over all religions.

GLOSSARY WORDS

Bunyānum Marṣūṣ, 'Īsa ibn Maryam, *Nūr(u) Allāh(i), Ṣaffan*

VOCABULARY

سورة الصَّفِ - ٦١

الركوع ١ - Section 1

بِسْمِ اللهِ ٱلرَّحْمٰنِ ٱلرَّحِيمِ

(١) سَبَّحَ لِلَّهِ	Glorifies Allah	(٣) كَبُرَ مَقْتًا	It is most hateful
مَا فِي	whatever is in	عِنْدَ اللهِ	in the sight of Allah
اَلسَّمٰوٰتِ	the heavens	أَنْ تَقُولُوا	that you say that
وَمَا فِي	and whatever is in	مَا لاَ تَفْعَلُونَ	which you do not do
اَلأَرْضِ	the earth	(٤) إِنَّ اللهَ يُحِبُّ	Surely! Allah loves
وَهُوَ الْعَزِيزُ	and He is the Mighty	الَّذِينَ يُقَاتِلُونَ	who fight
اَلْحَكِيمُ	the Wise	فِي سَبِيلِهِ	in His way
(٢) يَاأَيُّهَا الَّذِينَ	O you who	صَفًّا	in ranks
اٰمَنُوا	believe	كَأَنَّهُمْ	as if they were
لِمَ تَقُولُونَ	why say you	بُنْيَانٌ	wall
مَا لاَ تَفْعَلُونَ	which you do not do	مَرْصُوصٌ	solid

(٥) وَ إِذْ	And when	مُصَدِّقًا	verifying
قَالَ مُوسٰى	Moses said	لِمَا بَيْنَ يَدَىَّ	that which is before me
لِقَوْمِهِ	to his people	مِنَ التَّوْرٰىةِ	of the Torah
يٰقَوْمِ	O my people	وَمُبَشِّرًا	and giving the good news
لِمَ تُؤْذُونَنِى	why do you insult me	بِرَسُولٍ	of a Messenger
وَ قَدْ تَّعْلَمُونَ	when you know that	يَأْتِى	who will come
أَنِّى رَسُولُ اللهِ	that I am Allah's messenger	مِنْ بَعْدِى	after me
إِلَيْكُمْ	to you	اسْمُهُ أَحْمَدُ	his name being Ahmad
فَلَمَّا	but when	فَلَمَّا جَآءَهُمْ	and when he came to them
زَاغُوٓا	they deviated	بِالْبَيِّنٰتِ	with clear signs
أَزَاغَ اللهُ	Allah caused to deviate	قَالُوا هٰذَا	they said: This is
قُلُوبَهُمْ	their hearts	سِحْرٌ	enchantment, magic
وَ اللهُ لَا يَهْدِى	and Allah guides not	مُّبِينٌ	clear
الْقَوْمَ الْفٰسِقِينَ	the transgressing people	(٧) وَمَنْ أَظْلَمُ	And who is more unjust
(٦) وَ إِذْ	And when	مِمَّنِ افْتَرٰى	than who forges
قَالَ عِيسَى	Jesus said	عَلَى اللهِ	against Allah
ابْنُ مَرْيَمَ	Son of Mary	الْكَذِبَ	a lie
يٰبَنِىٓ إِسْرَآءِيلَ	O children of Israel	وَهُوَ يُدْعٰىٓ	And Allah invites
إِنِّى	Surely! I am	إِلَى الْإِسْلَامِ	to Islam
رَسُولُ اللهِ	the messenger of Allah	وَ اللهُ	and Allah
إِلَيْكُمْ	to you	لَا يَهْدِى	guides not

اَلقَوْمَ الظّٰلِمِينَ	the unjust people	أَرْسَلَ	sent
(٨) يُرِيدُونَ	They desire	رَسُولَهُ	His Messenger
لِيُطْفِئُوا	to put out	بِالْهُدٰى	with the guidance
نُورَ اللهِ	the light of Allah	وَ دِيْنِ الْحَقِّ	and the true religion
بِأَفْوَاهِهِمْ	with their mouths	لِيُظْهِرَهُ	that He may make it
واللّٰهُ مُتِمُّ	but Allah will perfect	عَلَى	overcome
نُورِهِ	His light	اَلدِّيْنِ	the religions
وَ لَوْ كَرِهَ	and though may be averse	كُلِّهِ	all of them
اَلْكٰفِرُونَ	the disbelievers	وَلَوْ كَرِهَ	and may be averse
(٩) هُوَ الَّذِى	He it is Who	اَلْمُشْرِكُونَ	the polytheists

Section 2: 10-14

SŪRAH AṢ-ṢAFF 61

The Battle Array / The Ranks

ARABIC TEXT

بِسۡمِ ٱللَّهِ ٱلرَّحۡمَٰنِ ٱلرَّحِيمِ

يَٰٓأَيُّهَا ٱلَّذِينَ ءَامَنُواْ هَلۡ أَدُلُّكُمۡ

عَلَىٰ تِجَٰرَةٖ تُنجِيكُم مِّنۡ عَذَابٍ أَلِيمٖ ١٠ تُؤۡمِنُونَ بِٱللَّهِ وَرَسُولِهِۦ وَتُجَٰهِدُونَ

فِي سَبِيلِ ٱللَّهِ بِأَمۡوَٰلِكُمۡ وَأَنفُسِكُمۡۚ ذَٰلِكُمۡ خَيۡرٞ لَّكُمۡ إِن كُنتُمۡ تَعۡلَمُونَ ١١

يَغۡفِرۡ لَكُمۡ ذُنُوبَكُمۡ وَيُدۡخِلۡكُمۡ جَنَّٰتٖ تَجۡرِي مِن تَحۡتِهَا ٱلۡأَنۡهَٰرُ وَمَسَٰكِنَ

طَيِّبَةٗ فِي جَنَّٰتِ عَدۡنٖۚ ذَٰلِكَ ٱلۡفَوۡزُ ٱلۡعَظِيمُ ١٢ وَأُخۡرَىٰ تُحِبُّونَهَاۖ نَصۡرٞ

مِّنَ ٱللَّهِ وَفَتۡحٞ قَرِيبٞۗ وَبَشِّرِ ٱلۡمُؤۡمِنِينَ ١٣ يَٰٓأَيُّهَا ٱلَّذِينَ ءَامَنُواْ كُونُوٓاْ

أَنصَارَ ٱللَّهِ كَمَا قَالَ عِيسَى ٱبۡنُ مَرۡيَمَ لِلۡحَوَارِيِّـۧنَ مَنۡ أَنصَارِيٓ إِلَى ٱللَّهِۖ

قَالَ ٱلۡحَوَارِيُّونَ نَحۡنُ أَنصَارُ ٱللَّهِۖ فَـَٔامَنَت طَّآئِفَةٞ مِّنۢ بَنِيٓ إِسۡرَٰٓءِيلَ

وَكَفَرَت طَّآئِفَةٞۖ فَأَيَّدۡنَا ٱلَّذِينَ ءَامَنُواْ عَلَىٰ عَدُوِّهِمۡ فَأَصۡبَحُواْ ظَٰهِرِينَ ١٤

TRANSLATIONS

10. O you who believe! shall I lead you to a bargain {*Tijārah*} that will save you from a grievous Penalty?

11. That you believe in Allāh and His Messenger, and that you strive (your utmost) in the Cause of Allāh {*Yujāhidūna*}, with your property and your persons: that will be best for you, if you but knew!

12. He will forgive you your sins, and admit you to Gardens {*Jannātin*} beneath which rivers flow, and to beautiful mansions in Gardens of Eternity: that is indeed the supreme Achievement.

13. And another (favor will He bestow), which you do love - help {*Naṣr*} from Allāh and a speedy victory: so give the Glad Tidings to the Believers.

14. O you who believe! Be you helpers of Allāh {*Anṣār Allah*}: as said Jesus, the son of Mary, to the Disciples, "Who will be my helpers {*Anṣārī*} to (the work of) Allāh?" Said the Disciples, "We are Allāh's helpers!" Then a portion of the Children of Israel believed, and a portion disbelieved: but We gave power to those who believed against their enemies, and they became the ones that prevailed.

(A. Y. Ali)

10. O you who believe! Shall I show you a commerce that will save you from a painful doom?

11. You should believe in Allāh and His messenger, and should strive for the cause of Allāh with your wealth and your lives. That is better for you, if you did but know.

12. He will forgive you your sins and bring you into Gardens underneath which rivers flow, and pleasant dwellings in Gardens of Eden. That is the supreme triumph.

13. And (He will give you) another blessing which you love: help from Allāh and present victory. Give good tidings (O Muhammad) to believers.

14. O you who believe! Be Allāh's helpers, even as Jesus son of Mary {`Īsā ibn Maryam} said unto the disciples: Who are my helpers for Allāh? They said: We are Allāh's helpers. And a party of the Children of Israel believed, while a party disbelieved. Then We strengthened those who believed against their foe, and they became the uppermost.

(M. M. Pickthal)

EXPLANATION (A. Y. Ali, revised)

10: *Tijārah* means trade, commerce and transaction: something offered or done in return for something we desire. What we give or do on our part is described in verse 11 below, and what we receive is described in verse 12. It is truly a wonderful bargain: what we are asked to give is so little, and what we are promised in return is so much.

11-12: It would indeed be a great bargain {*Tijārah*} to give so little and receive so much, if we only knew and understood the comparative value of things. We give up a few insignificant advantages, and in return, we gain the love and forgiveness of Allāh ﷻ and *Jannah* in the Hereafter.

13: The supreme achievement has already been mentioned: the Gardens of Eternity with Allāh ﷻ. A less remote achievement, which the people who first heard this Message could easily understand and appreciate, is help and victory. When working for a good cause, we have Allāh's help. No matter what odds are against us, we are sure of victory with Allāh's help.

14: If we seek Allāh's help, we must first help Allāh's Cause: that is, dedicate ourselves to Him entirely. This was also the teaching of Īsa عليه السلام, as mentioned in this verse.

Those Children of Israel who cared for truth believed in Īsa عليه السلام and followed his guidance. But the majority were hard-hearted and remained in their old ways, and maintained false racial pride. At first, the majority seemed to have the upper hand, when they thought they had crucified Īsa عليه السلام and killed his Message. But, they were soon brought to their senses. Jerusalem was destroyed by Titus in 70 A.D. and the Jews have been scattered ever since. Christianity became the major religion of the world until the beginning of Islam. It is promised to the people of Islam that they will succeed if they uphold the Truth and avoid the mistakes of the earlier believing communities.

IMPORTANT POINTS TO LEARN AND REFLECT UPON

- The believers are offered a trade {*Tijārah*} by Allāh ﷻ: that is, His pleasure in return of their obedience and struggle for His cause.
- The Muslims must respond to the call of Rasūlullāh ﷺ and be his *Anṣār* (Helpers) as were the followers of `Īsa ؑ.
- If Muslims become *Anṣār,* they will also succeed, as did the *Anṣār* of `Īsa ؑ.

GLOSSARY WORDS

Anṣār Allāh, Anṣārī, Jannātin, Naṣr, Tijārah, Yujāhidūna

VOCABULARY

الركوع ٢ - Section 2

بِسْمِ ٱللَّهِ ٱلرَّحْمَٰنِ ٱلرَّحِيمِ

(١٠) يَاأَيُّهَا الَّذِينَ	O you who	وَ تُجَاهِدُونَ	and strive hard
اٰمَنُوا	believe	فِى سَبِيلِ اللهِ	in Allah's way
هَلْ أدُلُّكُمْ	shall I lead you	بِأَمْوَالِكُمْ	with your wealth
عَلٰى تِجَارَةٍ	to a merchandise, trade	وَ أَنْفُسِكُمْ	and your lives
تُنْجِيكُمْ	which will deliver you	ذٰلِكُمْ خَيْرٌ لَّكُمْ	that is better for you
مِّنْ عَذَابٍ أَلِيمٍ	from a painful punishment	إِنْ كُنْتُمْ تَعْلَمُونَ	if you but know
(١١) تُؤْمِنُونَ بِاللهِ	You should believe in Allah	(١٢) يَغْفِرْ لَكُمْ	He will forgive you
وَرَسُولِه	and His Messenger	ذُنُوبَكُمْ	your sins

وَيُدْخِلْكُمْ	and cause you to enter	عِيسَى	Jesus
جَنّٰتٍ	Gardens, Jannah	اِبْنُ مَرْيَمَ	son of Mary
تَجْرِى	flow	لِلْحَوَارِيِّينَ	to the disciples
مِنْ تَحْتِهَا الْأَنْهٰرُ	beneath which rivers	مَنْ أَنْصَارِىَ	Who are my helpers
وَ مَسٰكِنَ طَيِّبَةً	and goodly dwellings	إِلَى اللهِ	in the cause of Allah
فِى جَنّٰتِ	in Gardens	قَالَ	said
عَدْنٍ	of perpetuity	اَلْحَوَارِيُّونَ	the disciples
ذٰلِكَ الْفَوْزُ	that is achievement	نَحْنُ أَنْصَارُ	we are helpers
اَلْعَظِيمُ	the mighty	اللهِ	of Allah
(١٣) وَ أُخْرٰى	And another	فَاٰمَنَتْ	believed
تُحِبُّونَهَا	you love it	طَّآئِفَةٌ	so a party
نَصْرٌ	help	مِنْ بَنِىَ	of the children
مِنَ اللهِ	from Allah	إِسْرَآءِيلَ	of Israel
وَفَتْحٌ	and a victory	وَكَفَرَتْ	disbelieved
قَرِيبٌ	near at hand	طَّآئِفَةٌ	and another party
وَ بَشِّرِ	and give good news	فَأَيَّدْنَا	then We aided
اَلْمُؤْمِنِينَ	to the believers	اَلَّذِينَ	those who
(١٤) يَٰأَيُّهَا الَّذِينَ	O you who	اٰمَنُوا	believed
اٰمَنُوا كُونُوآ	believe, be	عَلٰى عَدُوِّهِمْ	against their enemy
أَنْصَارَ اللهِ	helpers of Allah	فَأَصْبَحُوا	and they became
كَمَا قَالَ	as he said	ظٰهِرِينَ	predominant

Section 1: 1-8

سورة الجمعة

SŪRAH AL-JUMU‘AH 62: 1-11

Friday / The Congregation

Name: It is derived from the sentence, *"idhā nūdiya-li(a)ṣ-ṣalāti min yaumi (a)l-Jumu'ati"* of verse 9. In this *Sūrah,* injunctions are made about the *Jumu`ah* Prayer. It also covers other subjects.

Period of Revelation: The period of revelation of the first section (vv. 1-8) is A.H. 7, and was probably sent down on the occasion of the conquest of Khaiber or soon after it.

The second section (vv. 9-11) was revealed in the early Madīnah period. The incident mentioned in the last verse of this section must have happened at a time when people of Madīnah were not fully strengthened in their faith.

Theme and Subject Matter: The *Sūrah* consists of two separate parts that are logically connected to one another. The first section primarily addresses the Jews, allowing them reflect on the mission of Rasūlullāh ﷺ and their own failure to understand and grasp it. The second section describes the importance of *Jumu`ah* as a Muslim holy day. It is different from the Jewish Sabbath on Saturday. The rules of the two holy days are very different from each other.

It also teaches Muslims the spirit of *Ṣalāt al-Jumu`ah* and encourages them to inculcate habits of discipline and a firm faith in the bounty of Allāh ﷻ.

ARABIC TEXT

بِسْمِ اللَّهِ الرَّحْمَٰنِ الرَّحِيمِ

يُسَبِّحُ لِلَّهِ مَا فِي السَّمَٰوَٰتِ وَمَا فِي الْأَرْضِ الْمَلِكِ الْقُدُّوسِ الْعَزِيزِ
الْحَكِيمِ ﴿١﴾ هُوَ الَّذِي بَعَثَ فِي الْأُمِّيِّـۧنَ رَسُولًا مِّنْهُمْ يَتْلُوا
عَلَيْهِمْ ءَايَٰتِهِۦ وَيُزَكِّيهِمْ وَيُعَلِّمُهُمُ الْكِتَٰبَ وَالْحِكْمَةَ وَإِن كَانُوا
مِن قَبْلُ لَفِي ضَلَٰلٍ مُّبِينٍ ﴿٢﴾ وَءَاخَرِينَ مِنْهُمْ لَمَّا يَلْحَقُوا بِهِمْ ۚ
وَهُوَ الْعَزِيزُ الْحَكِيمُ ﴿٣﴾ ذَٰلِكَ فَضْلُ اللَّهِ يُؤْتِيهِ مَن يَشَآءُ ۚ وَاللَّهُ
ذُو الْفَضْلِ الْعَظِيمِ ﴿٤﴾ مَثَلُ الَّذِينَ حُمِّلُوا التَّوْرَىٰةَ ثُمَّ لَمْ
يَحْمِلُوهَا كَمَثَلِ الْحِمَارِ يَحْمِلُ أَسْفَارًا ۚ بِئْسَ مَثَلُ الْقَوْمِ
الَّذِينَ كَذَّبُوا بِـَٔايَٰتِ اللَّهِ ۚ وَاللَّهُ لَا يَهْدِي الْقَوْمَ الظَّٰلِمِينَ ﴿٥﴾
قُلْ يَٰٓأَيُّهَا الَّذِينَ هَادُوٓا إِن زَعَمْتُمْ أَنَّكُمْ أَوْلِيَآءُ لِلَّهِ مِن
دُونِ النَّاسِ فَتَمَنَّوُا الْمَوْتَ إِن كُنتُمْ صَٰدِقِينَ ﴿٦﴾ وَلَا يَتَمَنَّوْنَهُۥٓ
أَبَدًۢا بِمَا قَدَّمَتْ أَيْدِيهِمْ ۚ وَاللَّهُ عَلِيمٌۢ بِالظَّٰلِمِينَ ﴿٧﴾ قُلْ إِنَّ
الْمَوْتَ الَّذِي تَفِرُّونَ مِنْهُ فَإِنَّهُۥ مُلَٰقِيكُمْ ۖ ثُمَّ تُرَدُّونَ
إِلَىٰ عَٰلِمِ الْغَيْبِ وَالشَّهَٰدَةِ فَيُنَبِّئُكُم بِمَا كُنتُمْ تَعْمَلُونَ ﴿٨﴾

TRANSLATIONS

1. Whatever is in the heavens and on earth, does declare the Praises and Glory {*Yusabbi-ḥu*} of Allāh the Sovereign, the Holy One, the Exalted in Might, the Wise.

2. It is He Who has sent amongst the Unlettered {*'Ummiyyīn*} a messenger from among themselves, to rehearse to them His Signs, to sanctify them, and to instruct them in Scripture and Wisdom - although they had been, before, in manifest error -

3. As well as (to confer all these benefits upon) others of them, who have not already joined them: and He is Exalted in Might, Wise.

4. Such is the Bounty of Allāh, which He bestows on whom He will: and Allāh is the Lord of the highest bounty.

5. The similitude of those who were charged with the (obligations of the) Mosaic Law {*At-Tawrāt*}, but who subsequently failed in those (obligations), is that of a donkey which carries huge tomes {*Asfār*} (but understands them not). Evil is the similitude of people who falsify the Signs of Allāh: and Allāh guides not people who do wrong.

6. Say: "O you that stand on Judaism! If you think that you are friends to Allāh, to the exclusion of (other) men, then express your desire for Death, if you are truthful!"

7. But never will they express their desire (for Death), because of the (deeds) their

1. All that is in the heavens and all that is in the earth glorifies Allāh, the Sovereign Lord, the Holy One, the Mighty, the Wise.

2. He it is Who has sent among the unlettered ones a messenger of their own, to recite unto them His revelations and to make them grow, and to teach them the Scripture and Wisdom, though heretofore they were indeed in error manifest,

3. Along with others of them who have not yet joined them. He is the Mighty, the Wise.

4. That is the bounty of Allāh; which He gives unto whom He will. Allāh is of infinite bounty.

5. The likeness of those who are entrusted with the Law of Moses, yet apply it not, is as the likeness of the ass carrying books. Wretched is the likeness of folk who deny the revelations of Allāh. And Allāh guides not wrongdoing folk.

6. Say (O Muḥammad): O you who are Jews! If you claim that you are favored of Allāh apart from (all) mankind, then long for death if you are truthful.

7. But they will never long for it because of all that their own hands have sent hands have sent on before them! And Allāh knows well those that do wrong!

8. Say: "The Death from which you flee will truly overtake you: then will you be sent back to the Knower of things secret and open: and He will tell you (the truth of) the things that you did!"

(A. Y. Ali)

before, and Allāh is Aware of evil-doers.

8. Say (unto them, O Muḥammad): Lo! the death from which you shrink will surely meet you, and afterward you will be returned unto the Knower of the invisible and the visible, and He will tell you what you used to do.

(M. M. Pickthal)

EXPLANATION (A. Y. Ali, revised)

1: *Yusabbiḥū* ("Does declare the Praise and Glory") is used here to express an actual fact: 'Everything declares Praise and Glory of Allāh ﷻ because Allāh's Mercies extend to all His creatures. He sends His Revelation for the benefit of all, the ignorant and the educated alike.' Here, we have four of the Divine attributes of Allāh ﷻ: *Al-Malik* (The Sovereign), *Al-Quddūs* (The Holy), *Al-`Azīz* (The Mighty), and *Al-Ḥakīm* (The Wise). They are only four of the beautiful names of Allāh ﷻ mentioned in the Qur'ān and *Ḥadīth*.

2: {The mission of the Prophet ﷺ was authorized by Allāh ﷻ. Allāh ﷻ sent His messengers to all people. The uneducated and ignorant Arabs received the Last Prophet, who was from amongst their own people, and who delivered the universal Message. Though born among the Arabs, the mission of Rasūlullāh ﷺ was for all humankind.} The Messenger came as a teacher to a people who had never known Divine revelation before. He taught them how to recite the verses of the Qur'ān (*Tilāwah*), purified them (*Tazkiyah*) from their wrong beliefs and past sins, and taught (*Ta`līm*) them the Qur'ān and Wisdom (*Ḥikmah*). According to most commentators, the *Ḥikmah* is the *Sunnah* and *Ḥadīth* of Rasūlullāh ﷺ. The Unlettered *(al-'Ummiyyīn)* refers to the Arabs. In comparison to the People of the Book (the Jews and the Christians) who had a longer tradition of learning, the Arabs were illiterate. This shows that Allāh's Revelation is for the benefit of all people, whether they have worldly learning or not. {The miracle of the Revelation is that it made an unlettered person the final

Prophet and the greatest teacher of humanity; and made unlettered people the greatest moral and enlightened community. AG}

'Āyāti-hī (His Signs) are Allāh's wonderful Signs in His Creation and in His order of the world. It also includes the Verses of the Qur'ān, more specifically referred to here as "the Book" *(al-Kitāb)*.

Allāh سبحانه وتعالى is the Sovereign, and cares for all His subjects and has sent His Prophets and Messengers to them. He is the Holy One, Who purified those who were superstitious and wicked. He is Exalted in Power, and therefore, can send all these blessings to the most unlikely people. He is Wise, and therefore, instructs wisely, through written scriptures and in other ways. Previous ignorance or error is not held against a person or nation receiving the blessings of Allāh's Revelation, provided that such person or nation wants to be near to Allāh سبحانه وتعالى and pay attention to His Message.

3: "Others of them" refers to those other than his Arab people (non-Arabs of his time), as well as those who lived in other times. His message is relevant for all people and for all times.

4: The favor of sending a Messenger and revealing His Book is all a part of Allāh's Wise Will and Plan, and is also a Sign of His unlimited generosity to all.

5: The Children of Israel were chosen to receive Allāh's Message earlier in history. When their descendants changed the Message and became guilty of all the sins that the Prophets, such as Isaiah عليه السلام, warned them so strongly against, they became like beasts of burden, carrying wisdom on their backs, but unable to understand or profit from it. {In fact, this applies to any people who receive the Message and do not use it for their guidance; rather they make it a reason for national pride; they are no different than the beasts of burden. AG.}

6-7: Being a Jew is very different from being a faithful follower of the Law and Will of God. Any claim to be a chosen people and exemption from the responsibility of sharing the Message with others, or exemption from living by it, is pride: it is not in the spirit of the Message of Moses عليه السلام.

If the Jews claimed to be special friends of Allāh سبحانه وتعالى, why do they not eagerly desire death, which would bring them nearer to Allāh ﷻ? But of all people, they are the most desirous of this life and prefer the good things of this life to the Hereafter!

8: Before Allāh's Judgement seat, when Judgement is established, we will see the record of our all deeds committed in this world. Every one of our secret motives and visible actions will be accounted for.

IMPORTANT POINTS TO LEARN AND REFLECT UPON

- Allāh ﷻ sent the Messenger ﷺ to teach people to read and understand His Book, and to purify them from their wrong beliefs and deeds.
- If the people who received the Revelation, in this case the Jews, did not act upon its teachings; they were no better than the animals who (mindlessly) carry a load of books but do not benefit from it.
- The people who think that they are special friends of Allāh ﷻ must have a desire to meet Him, instead of being more desirous of this world.

GLOSSARY WORDS

Asfār, Sabbath, Similitude, *Tilāwah, Ummiyīn*

VOCABULARY

سورة اَلجُمُعَة - ١١٠

الركوع ١ - Section 1

بِسْمِ اللهِ الرَّحْمٰنِ الرَّحِيمِ

(١) يُسَبِّحُ لِلّٰهِ	Glorifies Allah	وَمَا فِى	and whatever is in
مَا فِى	whatever is in	الأَرْضِ	the earth
السَّمٰوٰتِ	the heavens	المَلِكِ	the King

القُدُّوسِ	the Holy	الحَكِيمُ	the Wise
العَزِيزِ	the Mighty	(٤) ذٰلِكَ	That is
الحَكِيمِ	the Wise	فَضْلُ اللهِ	Allah's grace
(٢) هُوَ الَّذِى	He it is Who	يُؤْتِيهِ	He grants it
بَعَثَ	raised	مَنْ يَّشَآءُ	to whom He pleases
فِى الْأُمِّيّٖنَ	among the illiterates	وَ اللهُ	And Allah
رَسُولاً	a Messenger	ذُو الْفَضْلِ العَظِيمِ	the lord of Mighty Grace
مِّنْهُمْ	from among themselves	(٥) مَثَلُ الَّذِينَ	The likeness of those
يَتْلُوا	who recites	حُمِّلُوا	who were charged
عَلَيْهِمْ اٰيٰتِهِ	to them His revelations	التَّوْرٰةَ	with the Torah
وَ يُزَكِّيهِمْ	and purifies them	ثُمَّ لَمْ يَحْمِلُوهَا	then they observed it not
وَ يُعَلِّمُهُمُ	and teaches them	كَمَثَلِ	is as the likeness
الكِتٰبَ	the Book	الْحِمَارِ	the ass
وَ الْحِكْمَةَ	and the Wisdom	يَحْمِلُ أَسْفَارًا	carrying books
وَ إِنْ كَانُوا	although they were	بِئْسَ	Evil is
مِنْ قَبْلُ	before	مَثَلُ الْقَوْمِ	the likeness of the people
لَفِى ضَلٰلٍ	in manifest error	الَّذِينَ كَذَّبُوا	who reject
مُّبِينٍ	certainly	بِاٰيَاتِ اللهِ	the signs of Allah
(٣) وَّ اٰخَرِينَ	And others	وَ اللهُ	and Allah
مِنْهُمْ	among them	لاَ يَهْدِى	guides not
لَمَّا يَلْحَقُوا	who have not yet joined	القَوْمَ الظّٰلِمِينَ	the iniquitous people
بِهِمْ	them	(٦) قُلْ يٰأَيُّهَا الَّذِينَ	Say: O you who
وَهُوَ الْعَزِيزُ	He is the Mighty	هَادُوآ	are Jews

إِنْ زَعَمْتُمْ	if you think that	صٰدِقِينَ	truthful
أَنَّكُمْ	you are	(٧) وَ لَا يَتَمَنَّوْنَهُ	But they will not invoke it
أَوْلِيَآءُ لِلّٰهِ	the favorites of Allah	أَبَدًا	never
مِنْ دُونِ	to the exclusion	بِمَا قَدَّمَتْ	of what was sent before
اَلنَّاسِ	of other people	أَيْدِيهِمْ	their hands
فَتَمَنَّوُا	then invoke	وَ اللّٰهُ	and Allah is
اَلْمَوْتَ	the death	عَلِيمٌ	the Knower
إِنْ كُنْتُمْ	if you are	بِالظّٰلِمِينَ	of the wrongdoers

Section 2:9-11

SŪRAH AL-JUMU‘AH 62

Friday / The Congregation

ARABIC TEXT

بِسْمِ ٱللَّهِ ٱلرَّحْمَٰنِ ٱلرَّحِيمِ

يَٰٓأَيُّهَا ٱلَّذِينَ ءَامَنُوٓاْ إِذَا نُودِىَ لِلصَّلَوٰةِ مِن يَوْمِ ٱلْجُمُعَةِ
فَٱسْعَوْاْ إِلَىٰ ذِكْرِ ٱللَّهِ وَذَرُواْ ٱلْبَيْعَ ذَٰلِكُمْ خَيْرٌ لَّكُمْ إِن كُنتُمْ
تَعْلَمُونَ ﴿٩﴾ فَإِذَا قُضِيَتِ ٱلصَّلَوٰةُ فَٱنتَشِرُواْ فِى ٱلْأَرْضِ
وَٱبْتَغُواْ مِن فَضْلِ ٱللَّهِ وَٱذْكُرُواْ ٱللَّهَ كَثِيرًا لَّعَلَّكُمْ تُفْلِحُونَ
﴿١٠﴾ وَإِذَا رَأَوْاْ تِجَٰرَةً أَوْ لَهْوًا ٱنفَضُّوٓاْ إِلَيْهَا وَتَرَكُوكَ قَآئِمًا قُلْ
مَا عِندَ ٱللَّهِ خَيْرٌ مِّنَ ٱللَّهْوِ وَمِنَ ٱلتِّجَٰرَةِ وَٱللَّهُ خَيْرُ ٱلرَّٰزِقِينَ ﴿١١﴾

TRANSLATIONS

9. O you who believe! When the call is proclaimed to prayer {*Ṣalāh*} on Friday (the Day of Assembly), hasten earnestly to the Remembrance of Allāh {*Dhikri (A)llah*}, and leave off business (and traffic): that is best for you if you but knew!

9. O you who believe! When the call is heard for the prayer of the day of congregation, haste unto remembrance of Allāh and leave your trading. That is better for you if you did but know.

10. And when the prayer is finished, then may you disperse through the land, and seek of the Bounty of Allāh {*Faḍli(A)llāh*}: and celebrate the Praises of Allāh often (and without stint): that you may prosper.

11. But when they see some bargain {*Tijārah*} or some amusement {*Lahw*}, they disperse headlong to it, and leave you standing. Say: "The (blessing) from the Presence of Allāh is better than any amusement or bargain! And Allāh is the Best to provide (for all needs)."

(A. Y. Ali)

10. And when the prayer is ended, then disperse in the land and seek of Allāh's bounty, and remember Allāh much, that you may be successful.

11. But when they spy some merchandise or pastime they break away to it and leave you standing. Say: That which Allāh has is better than pastime and than merchandise, and Allāh is the best of providers.

(M. M. Pickthal)

EXPLANATION (A. Y. Ali, revised)

9: Friday is the Day of Assembly, the weekly meeting of the Congregation, when Muslims show their unity through common public worship. It is preceded by a Khutbah (Sermon), in which the *'Imām* (the leader) reviews the community's week, and offers advice on righteous Islamic living. Islam is a religion of unity and strives to bring the community together. The gradual social relations of Muslims develop as we follow the teachings of Islam in these ways:

(1) Each individual remembers Allāh ﷻ for himself or herself five or more times everyday in the home or in the mosque.

(2) Every Friday there is a bigger congregation in the central mosque *(Jām'i)*.

(3) Each year, at the two *'Īdain, 'Īd al-Fitr and 'Īd al-'Aḍḥā,* there is one large congregation at one center in each city or neighborhood.

(4) At least once in a lifetime, whenever possible, a Muslim shares in the vast international assembly of the world for *Ḥajj*, the pilgrimage to Makkah.

The idea behind the Islamic weekly "Day of Assembly" differs from that behind the Jewish *Sabbath* (Saturday) or the Christian Sunday. The Jewish *Sabbath* is primarily a remembrance of Allāh ﷻ completing His work and resting on the seventh day (Genesis 2:2; Exodus 20:11). The Qur'ān teaches us that Allāh ﷻ needs no rest, nor does He feel fatigue (*Al-Baqarah* 2:255).

The Jews forbid work on that day, but say nothing about worship or prayer (Exodus 20:10). Our teaching says: 'When the time for *Jumu`ah* Prayer comes, close your business and answer the summons loyally and earnestly. When the meeting is over, go about your business.'

10: Prosperity is not to be measured by wealth or worldly gains. There is greater prosperity in the health of mind and spirit.

11: Do not be distracted by the craze for amusement or worldly gain. If you lead a righteous and sober life, Allāh ﷻ will provide for you better than any provision you can possibly imagine.

IMPORTANT POINTS TO LEARN AND REFLECT UPON

- The Believers must halt their business and other activities when they hear the *'Adhān* and rush for the *Ṣalāh* of *Jumu`ah.*
- After the *Ṣalāh,* they are free to return to their work or other engagements.
- We must not run after worldly gain, ignoring our religious obligations: we must remember that Allāh ﷻ is the Best Provider of all.

GLOSSARY WORDS

Dhikr(u)Allāh, Faḍl, 'Īdain, Khutbah, Lahw, Tijārah

VOCABULARY

٢ - الركوع - Section 2

بِسْمِ ٱللَّهِ ٱلرَّحْمٰنِ ٱلرَّحِيمِ

(٨) قُلْ	Say
إِنَّ الْمَوْتَ	verily, the death which
اَلَّذِي تَفِرُّونَ مِنْهُ	from you flee
فَإِنَّهُ	that will surely
مُلٰقِيكُمْ	overtake you
ثُمَّ تُرَدُّونَ	then you will be returned
إِلٰى	to
عٰلِمِ	the Knower
اَلغَيْبِ	of the unseen
وَ الشَّهَادَةِ	and the seen
فَيُنَبِّئُكُمْ	so He will inform you
بِمَا كُنْتُمْ	of that which
تَعْمَلُونَ	you did
(٩) يٰأَيُّهَا الَّذِينَ	O you who
اٰمَنُوآ	believe
إِذَا نُودِيَ	when the call is sounded
لِلصَّلٰوةِ	for prayer
مِنْ يَوْمِ الْجُمُعَةِ	on Friday
فَاسْعَوْا	hasten
إِلٰى	to
ذِكْرِ اللهِ	the remembrance of Allah
وَذَرُوا الْبَيْعَ	and leave off business
ذٰلِكُمْ	that is
خَيْرٌ لَّكُمْ	better for you
إِنْ كُنْتُمْ تَعْلَمُونَ	if you know
(١٠) فَإِذَا	But when
قُضِيَتِ	is ended
اَلصَّلٰوةُ	the prayer
فَانْتَشِرُوا	disperse abroad
فِي الْأَرْضِ	in the land
وَابْتَغُوا	and seek
مِنْ فَضْلِ اللهِ	of Allah's Grace
وَ اذْكُرُوا اللهَ	and remember Allah
كَثِيرًا	much
لَعَلَّكُمْ	that you may be
تُفْلِحُونَ	successful
(١١) وَ إِذَا رَأَوْا	And when they see
تِجَارَةً	merchandise, trade

أَوْ لَهْوَ	or sport	خَيْرٌ	is better
انْفَضُّوَا إِلَيْهَا	they break away to it	مِّنَ اللَّهْوِ	than sport
وَ تَرَكُوكَ	and leave you	وَمِنَ التِّجَارَةِ	and merchandise, trade
قَآئِمًا	standing	وَ اللهُ	and Allah
قُلْ مَا	Say: what is	خَيْرُ	is the best
عِنْدَ اللهِ	with Allah	اَلرّٰزِقِينَ	of Providers

Section 1:1-14

سُورَةُ المُلْكِ

SŪRAH AL-MULK 67: 1-30

The Dominion / The Sovereignty

Name: The *Sūrah* takes its name *al-Mulk* from the very first verse, *Subḥān alladhī bi-yadihi (a)l-Mulk. Al-Mulk* means Sovereignty, Power, Supreme rule; it belongs to Allāh ﷿.

Period of Revelation: It is not known from any authentic tradition when this *Sūrah* was revealed, but the subject matter and style indicate that it is one of the earliest Makkan *Sūrahs*.

Theme and Subject Matter: In this *Sūrah*, the teachings of Islam are introduced briefly. The people living in ignorance are invited to the truth.

In the first five verses, we are informed that Allāh ﷿ has created a well-organized and flawless universe. The creations of Allāh ﷿ have a purpose, and it is our responsibility to live according to true Divine Revelation.

In verses 6-11, people are warned of the evil consequences of their disbelief and punishment in the Hereafter.

In verses 12-14, Allāh ﷿ knows all His creation and is well aware of all that is open and hidden. One should worship Allāh ﷿ alone, avoid evil, and fear accountability for their actions in the Hereafter. Those who believe and lead a righteous life will earn forgiveness and earn Allāh's pleasure in the Hereafter.

In verses 15-23, an appeal is made to human intelligence and common sense, using examples of Allāh's many blessings. The earth on which we walk, with full satisfaction and peace of mind, and from which we obtain our sustenance, has been made to serve our means. Human beings are invited to observe nature, and how the Divine laws operate ("See the flight of the birds"). We are asked to use our sight, our hearing and our minds to recognize the Sovereignty of our Lord through His many Blessings and Signs.

In verses 24-27, it is not for the Prophet ﷺ to inform us about the time of the Day of Judgement. It is a reality, and it is sure to come. It will come suddenly, without warning.

In verses 28-29, the disbelievers curse the Holy Prophet ﷺ and pray for his (and the believers') destruction. They are warned to take care of themselves. The time would surely come when truth will be made clear to everyone.

Finally, a simple question is asked to make people reflect upon the fact that their lives are totally dependent on Allāh's Mercy: "If the water, the source of all your life, should disappear, who has the power to restore this source to you?"

ARABIC TEXT

بِسْمِ ٱللَّهِ ٱلرَّحْمَٰنِ ٱلرَّحِيمِ

تَبَٰرَكَ ٱلَّذِى بِيَدِهِ ٱلْمُلْكُ وَهُوَ عَلَىٰ كُلِّ شَىْءٍ قَدِيرٌ ﴿١﴾ ٱلَّذِى خَلَقَ
ٱلْمَوْتَ وَٱلْحَيَوٰةَ لِيَبْلُوَكُمْ أَيُّكُمْ أَحْسَنُ عَمَلًا ۚ وَهُوَ ٱلْعَزِيزُ ٱلْغَفُورُ ﴿٢﴾
ٱلَّذِى خَلَقَ سَبْعَ سَمَٰوَٰتٍ طِبَاقًا ۖ مَّا تَرَىٰ فِى خَلْقِ ٱلرَّحْمَٰنِ مِن
تَفَٰوُتٍ ۖ فَٱرْجِعِ ٱلْبَصَرَ هَلْ تَرَىٰ مِن فُطُورٍ ﴿٣﴾ ثُمَّ ٱرْجِعِ ٱلْبَصَرَ كَرَّتَيْنِ
يَنقَلِبْ إِلَيْكَ ٱلْبَصَرُ خَاسِئًا وَهُوَ حَسِيرٌ ﴿٤﴾ وَلَقَدْ زَيَّنَّا ٱلسَّمَآءَ
ٱلدُّنْيَا بِمَصَٰبِيحَ وَجَعَلْنَٰهَا رُجُومًا لِّلشَّيَٰطِينِ ۖ وَأَعْتَدْنَا لَهُمْ عَذَابَ

السَّعِيرِ ﴿٥﴾ وَلِلَّذِينَ كَفَرُوا بِرَبِّهِمْ عَذَابُ جَهَنَّمَ ۖ وَبِئْسَ الْمَصِيرُ
﴿٦﴾ إِذَا أُلْقُوا فِيهَا سَمِعُوا لَهَا شَهِيقًا وَهِيَ تَفُورُ ﴿٧﴾ تَكَادُ تَمَيَّزُ
مِنَ الْغَيْظِ ۖ كُلَّمَا أُلْقِيَ فِيهَا فَوْجٌ سَأَلَهُمْ خَزَنَتُهَا أَلَمْ يَأْتِكُمْ نَذِيرٌ ﴿٨﴾
قَالُوا بَلَىٰ قَدْ جَاءَنَا نَذِيرٌ فَكَذَّبْنَا وَقُلْنَا مَا نَزَّلَ اللَّهُ مِنْ شَيْءٍ إِنْ أَنْتُمْ
إِلَّا فِي ضَلَالٍ كَبِيرٍ ﴿٩﴾ وَقَالُوا لَوْ كُنَّا نَسْمَعُ أَوْ نَعْقِلُ مَا كُنَّا فِي أَصْحَابِ
السَّعِيرِ ﴿١٠﴾ فَاعْتَرَفُوا بِذَنْبِهِمْ فَسُحْقًا لِأَصْحَابِ السَّعِيرِ ﴿١١﴾
إِنَّ الَّذِينَ يَخْشَوْنَ رَبَّهُمْ بِالْغَيْبِ لَهُمْ مَغْفِرَةٌ وَأَجْرٌ كَبِيرٌ ﴿١٢﴾
وَأَسِرُّوا قَوْلَكُمْ أَوِ اجْهَرُوا بِهِ ۖ إِنَّهُ عَلِيمٌ بِذَاتِ الصُّدُورِ ﴿١٣﴾ أَلَا
يَعْلَمُ مَنْ خَلَقَ وَهُوَ اللَّطِيفُ الْخَبِيرُ ﴿١٤﴾

TRANSLATIONS

1. Blessed be He in Whose hands is Dominion {*al-Mulk*}; and He over all things Has Power.

2. He Who created Death and Life, that He may try which of you is best in deed; and He is the Exalted in Might, Oft-Forgiving -

1. Blessed is He in Whose hand is the Sovereignty, and He is Able to do all things -

2. Who has created life and death that He may try you, which of you is best in conduct; and He is the Mighty, Forgiving,

3. He Who created the seven heavens one above another: no want of proportion will you see in the Creation of (Allāh) Most Gracious. So turn your vision again: See you any flaw?

4. Again turn your vision a second time: (your) vision will come back to you dull and discomfited, in a state worn out.

5. And We have, (from of old), adorned the lowest heaven with Lamps, and We have made such (Lamps) (as) missiles to drive away the Evil Ones, and have prepared for them the Penalty of the Blazing Fire.

6. For those who reject their Lord (and Cherisher) is the Penalty of Hell: and evil is (such) destination.

7. When they are cast therein, they will hear the (terrible) drawing in of its breath {Shahīq} even as it blazes forth {*Tafūr*},

8. Almost bursting with fury: every time a Group is cast therein, its Keepers will ask "Did no Warner come to you?"

9. They will say: "Yes indeed; a Warner did come to us, but we rejected him and said, 'Allāh never sent down any (Message): you are in nothing but an egregious delusion!'"

10. They will further say: "Had we but listened or used our intelligence, we should not (now) be among the Companions of the Blazing Fire!"

3. Who has created seven heavens in harmony. You (Muḥammad) can see no fault in the Beneficent One's creation; then look again: Can you see any rifts?

4. Then look again and yet again, your sight will return unto you weakened and made dim.

5. And verily We have beautified the world's heaven with lamps, and We have made them missiles for the devils and for them We have prepared the doom of flame.

6. And for those who disbelieve in their Lord there is the doom of hell, a hapless journey's end!

7. When they are flung therein they hear its roaring as it boils up,

8. As it would burst with rage. Whenever a (fresh) host flung therein the wardens thereof ask them: Came there unto you no warner?

9. They say: Yes, verily, a warner came unto us; but we denied and said: Allāh has naught revealed; you are in naught but a great error.

10. And they say: Had we been wont to listen or have sense, we had not been among the dwellers in the flames.

11. They will then confess their sins: but far will be (Forgiveness) from the Companions of the Blazing Fire!

12. As for those who fear their Lord unseen, for them is Forgiveness and a great Reward.

13. And whether you hide your word or publish it, He certainly has (full) knowledge, of the secrets of (all) hearts.

14. Should He not know - He that created? And He is the One that understands the finest mysteries {*Al-Laṭīf*} (and) is Well-Acquainted (with them) {*Al-Khabīr*}.

(A. Y. Ali)

11. So they acknowledge their sins; but far removed (from mercy) are the dwellers in the flames.

12. Lo! those who fear their Lord in secret, theirs will be forgiveness and a great reward.

13. And keep your opinion secret or proclaim it, lo! He is Knower of all that is in the breasts (of men).

14. Should He not know what He created? And He is the Subtle {*Al-Laṭīf*}, the Aware {*Al-Khabīr*}.

(M. M. Pickthal)

EXPLANATION (A. Y. Ali, revised)

1: What do we mean when we bless the name of Allāh ﷻ, or proclaim that the whole creation should bless the name of the Lord? We mean that we recognize and proclaim His Mercy to us. All blessings and happiness are through Him.

The Dominion, *Al-Mulk,* means Sovereignty; the right to carry out His Will. The Power, *Al-Qudrah,* is the capacity to carry out His Will, so that nothing can resist or check it. Allāh ﷻ is Lord of both the visible and invisible worlds.

2: "Created Death and Life." In this verse, Death is put before Life; it is created. In *Al-Baqarah* 2:28 we read: "Seeing that you were without life (literally, dead), and He gave you life; then will He cause you to die, and will again bring you to life; and again to Him will you return."

Thus, death, is:

(1) The state before life began

(2) The state in which life as we know it ceases

The next stage will be the Day of Judgement, and the final stage will be new, eternal life. Clearly, our present life is given to us so that we may strive to reach a more noble state after death. All this is possible because Allāh ﷻ is so Exalted in Might that He can perfectly carry out His Will and Purpose. His Purpose is to guide His servants to His Mercy and Goodness through His Revelations.

3: What we are concerned with here is the order and beauty of the vast spaces and marvelous bodies that follow regular laws of motion in the visible world. From these, we are to form some idea of the even greater invisible world. To gain insight into that {useen} world, we need special spiritual vision. {In this life, we are unable to fully grasp that vision. We have to depend on Revelation and prayers for its understanding. AG}

4: Regarding the external, visible world, we are asked to observe and study it thoroughly, as deeply as our understanding will allow. However, as close as we observe it, we shall find no flaw in it. It is our own powers of reason and logic that fail to go beyond a certain limit.

5: "Lowest (or nearest) heaven" is the one visible to our eyes through the stars. Lamps are in reference to fixed stars, planets, comets, shooting stars, etc. On a clear night, the beauty of the star-studded heavens is undeniable. Here, they illustrate two points:

(1) Their beauty, groupings and motions shows the Harmony of the One True Creator

(2) The Power and Glory behind their beauty shows that Allāh ﷻ has appointed guards to safeguard them from the attack of evil.

The good in Allāh's world is protected against every assault of evil. Evil is not part of the heavenly system. Whenever evil sneaks in, it is repulsed and pursued by a flaming fire. The piercing trail of a shooting star gives us some visible idea of the struggle in our physical world. {This note is based upon Ali's commentary on *Aṣ-Ṣāffāt* 37:6-10 and *Al-Ḥijr* 15:16-18. AG}

6: The light of the stars suggests the beauty and order of the external world; yet, when it meets with resistance it can self-destruct. Thus, in the moral and spiritual world, disharmony and rebellion against our Cherisher and Sustainer, from Whom we receive nothing but goodness, destroys our spiritual happiness. The punishment, then, is Fire in its fiercest intensity.

7: Shahīq means 'the emission of a deep breath.' The verb *fara* means 'to blaze forth, to gush forth.' The flames which the fire throws out have a fierce aggressiveness.

8: Pure and innocent Nature does not recognize the crookedness of human evil, and it is surprised by so many human beings coming in for punishment. It wonders if no warning was given to humans. On the contrary, humans were warned by clear signs, through Revelations and through their own God-given conscience.

9: Allāh's Signs were not only rejected and defied, but the righteous people and prophets were persecuted and mocked (See also *Yā Sīn* 36:30).

10: Humans have been given the power to distinguish good from evil, and they are further helped by the teachings of the great messengers. It is the failure to follow the Revelation, despite our true nature, that leads to our degradation and destruction.

11: {On the Day of Judgement} reality will be made clear to the *Kuffār*. They will be unable to offer excuses for their sins. At last, they will confess their sins freely, but this will not be considered repentance. True repentance involves a person's willingness to change; and the time for change will have long passed.

12: Fear of Allāh ﷻ is borne out of our intense love for Him. Out of love for Him, we fear doing anything against His Will. We love Him intensely in our hearts, even though we do not see Him with our bodily senses. Such intensity of love earns forgiveness for any past sins, and is rewarded with Allāh's Love and Mercy. (See also *Fāṭir* 35:18 and note)

13-14: Allāh ﷻ is the Creator, and thus, He knows His own creations intimately. However, we cannot comprehend the extent of His knowledge, as our own knowledge is so limited. His knowledge is further characterized by His understanding of the deepest mysteries (*al-Laṭīf*) and being well-acquainted with them (*al-Khabīr*). (See also *Al-Ḥajj* 22:63. note)

IMPORTANT POINTS TO LEARN AND REFLECT UPON

- Allāh ﷻ has created life and death to test who, among His servants, is best in deeds.
- Allāh ﷻ has created everything in due proportion; and all His creation has a purpose.
- Allāh's Laws of reward and punishment are based upon His justice.

GLOSSARY WORDS

al-Mulk, degradation, disharmony, grasp, harmony, *Shahīq*

VOCABULARY

سورة الملك - ٣٠

الركوع ١ - Section 1

بِسْمِ ٱللَّهِ ٱلرَّحْمٰنِ ٱلرَّحِيمِ

(١) تَبٰرَكَ	Blessed be He	لِيَبْلُوَكُمْ أَيُّكُمْ	in order to try which of you
الَّذِى بِيَدِهِ	in Whose Hands	أَحْسَنُ عَمَلاً	is best in deed
الْمُلْكُ	the Dominion, the Sovereignty	وَهُوَ الْعَزِيزُ الْغَفُورُ	and He is the Exalted in Might
وَ هُوَ عَلَى كُلِّ شَيْءٍ	and He over all things	(٣) الَّذِى خَلَقَ	He Who created
قَدِيرٌ	has power	سَبْعَ سَمٰوٰتٍ	seven heavens
(٢) الَّذِى خَلَقَ	He Who created	طِبَاقًا	one above the other
الْمَوْتَ	the death	مَا تَرٰى	will you see not
وَ الْحَيٰوةَ	and the life	فِى خَلْقِ الرَّحْمٰنِ	in the creation of the Most Gracious

مِنْ تَفٰوُتٍ	want of proportion	عَذَابُ جَهَنَّمَ	the penalty of Hell
فَارْجِعِ الْبَصَرَ	so turn your vision	وَبِئْسَ الْمَصِيرُ	and evil is (their) destination
هَلْ تَرٰى	do you see	(٧) إِذَآ أُلْقُوا فِيهَا	When they are cast therein
مِنْ فُطُورٍ	any flaw, defect	سَمِعُوا لَهَا	they will hear its
(٤) ثُمَّ ارْجِعِ الْبَصَرَ	Again, turn your vision	شَهِيقًا	terrible drawing in of breath
كَرَّتَيْنِ	a second time	وَهِيَ تَفُورُ	even as it blazes forth
يَنْقَلِبْ إِلَيْكَ	will come back to you	(٨) تَكَادُ تَمَيَّزُ	Almost bursting
الْبَصَرُ خَاسِئًا	your vision dull and weak	مِنَ الْغَيْظِ	with fury
وَهُوَ حَسِيرٌ	in a state worn out	كُلَّمَآ أُلْقِيَ فِيهَا	every time is cast therein
(٥) وَ لَقَدْ زَيَّنَّا	And We have adorned	فَوْجٌ	a group
اَلسَّمَآءَ الدُّنْيَا	the lowest heaven	سَأَلَهُمْ	will ask them
بِمَصَابِيحَ	with lamps	خَزَنَتُهَا	its keepers
وَجَعَلْنٰهَا	and We have made it	أَلَمْ يَأْتِكُمْ نَذِيرٌ	did no warner come to you
رُجُومًا	(as) missiles to drive away	(٩) قَالُوا	They will say
لِّلشَّيٰطِينِ	Satans	بَلٰى قَدْ جَآءَنَا	yes it did come to us
وَ أَعْتَدْنَا	and We have prepared	نَذِيرٌ فَكَذَّبْنَا	a warner but we rejected him
لَهُمْ	for them	وَ قُلْنَا	and We said
عَذَابَ	the penalty of	مَا نَزَّلَ اللهُ	Allah never sent down
اَلسَّعِيرِ	the Blazing Fire	مِنْ شَيْءٍ إِنْ أَنْتُمْ	any (Message), you are
(٦) وَ لِلَّذِينَ كَفَرُوا	For those who reject	إِلَّا فِي ضَلٰلٍ كَبِيرٍ	but in a grave error
بِرَبِّهِمْ	their Lord	(١٠) وَ قَالُوا	And they will further say

لَوْ كُنَّا نَسْمَعُ	had we but listened
أَوْ نَعْقِلُ	or used our intelligence
مَا كُنَّا	we should not be
فِي أَصْحٰبِ	among companions
السَّعِيرِ	of Blazing Fire
(١١) فَاعْتَرَفُوا	They will then confess
بِذَنْبِهِمْ	their sin
فَسُحْقًا	but far from Allah's mercy
لِأَصْحٰبِ	the companions
السَّعِيرِ	of the Blazing Fire
(١٢) إِنَّ الَّذِينَ	As for those who
يَخْشَوْنَ	they fear
رَبَّهُمْ بِالْغَيْبِ	their Lord unseen

لَهُمْ مَغْفِرَةٌ	for them is forgiveness
وَّ أَجْرٌ كَبِيرٌ	and a great reward
(١٣) وَ أَسِرُّوا	And whether you hide
قَوْلَكُمْ	your word
أَوِ اجْهَرُوا بِهِ	or publicize it
إِنَّهُ	He certainly
عَلِيمٌ	has knowledge
بِذَاتِ الصُّدُورِ	of the secrets of hearts
(١٤) أَلَا يَعْلَمُ	Should He not know
مَنْ خَلَقَ	He that created
وَ هُوَ	and He is the One
اللَّطِيفُ	Who understands the finest mysteries
الْخَبِيرُ	well acquainted (with them)

Section 2:15-30

SŪRAH AL-MULK 67

The Dominion / The Sovereignty

ARABIC TEXT

بِسْمِ ٱللَّهِ ٱلرَّحْمَٰنِ ٱلرَّحِيمِ

هُوَ ٱلَّذِى جَعَلَ لَكُمُ

ٱلْأَرْضَ ذَلُولًا فَٱمْشُوا۟ فِى مَنَاكِبِهَا وَكُلُوا۟ مِن رِّزْقِهِۦ ۖ وَإِلَيْهِ ٱلنُّشُورُ

﴿١٥﴾ ءَأَمِنتُم مَّن فِى ٱلسَّمَآءِ أَن يَخْسِفَ بِكُمُ ٱلْأَرْضَ فَإِذَا هِىَ

تَمُورُ ﴿١٦﴾ أَمْ أَمِنتُم مَّن فِى ٱلسَّمَآءِ أَن يُرْسِلَ عَلَيْكُمْ حَاصِبًا ۖ

فَسَتَعْلَمُونَ كَيْفَ نَذِيرِ ﴿١٧﴾ وَلَقَدْ كَذَّبَ ٱلَّذِينَ مِن قَبْلِهِمْ فَكَيْفَ

كَانَ نَكِيرِ ﴿١٨﴾ أَوَلَمْ يَرَوْا۟ إِلَى ٱلطَّيْرِ فَوْقَهُمْ صَٰٓفَّٰتٍ وَيَقْبِضْنَ ۚ مَا

يُمْسِكُهُنَّ إِلَّا ٱلرَّحْمَٰنُ ۚ إِنَّهُۥ بِكُلِّ شَىْءٍۭ بَصِيرٌ ﴿١٩﴾ أَمَّنْ هَٰذَا ٱلَّذِى

هُوَ جُندٌ لَّكُمْ يَنصُرُكُم مِّن دُونِ ٱلرَّحْمَٰنِ ۚ إِنِ ٱلْكَٰفِرُونَ إِلَّا فِى غُرُورٍ

﴿٢٠﴾ أَمَّنْ هَٰذَا ٱلَّذِى يَرْزُقُكُمْ إِنْ أَمْسَكَ رِزْقَهُۥ ۚ بَل لَّجُّوا۟ فِى عُتُوٍّ

وَنُفُورٍ ﴿٢١﴾ أَفَمَن يَمْشِى مُكِبًّا عَلَىٰ وَجْهِهِۦٓ أَهْدَىٰٓ أَمَّن يَمْشِى سَوِيًّا

عَلَىٰ صِرَٰطٍ مُّسْتَقِيمٍ ﴿٢٢﴾ قُلْ هُوَ ٱلَّذِىٓ أَنشَأَكُمْ وَجَعَلَ لَكُمُ ٱلسَّمْعَ

وَٱلْأَبْصَٰرَ وَٱلْأَفْـِٔدَةَ ۖ قَلِيلًا مَّا تَشْكُرُونَ ﴿٢٣﴾ قُلْ هُوَ ٱلَّذِى ذَرَأَكُمْ
فِى ٱلْأَرْضِ وَإِلَيْهِ تُحْشَرُونَ ﴿٢٤﴾ وَيَقُولُونَ مَتَىٰ هَٰذَا ٱلْوَعْدُ إِن كُنتُمْ
صَٰدِقِينَ ﴿٢٥﴾ قُلْ إِنَّمَا ٱلْعِلْمُ عِندَ ٱللَّهِ وَإِنَّمَآ أَنَا۠ نَذِيرٌ مُّبِينٌ ﴿٢٦﴾
فَلَمَّا رَأَوْهُ زُلْفَةً سِيٓـَٔتْ وُجُوهُ ٱلَّذِينَ كَفَرُوا۟ وَقِيلَ هَٰذَا ٱلَّذِى
كُنتُم بِهِۦ تَدَّعُونَ ﴿٢٧﴾ قُلْ أَرَءَيْتُمْ إِنْ أَهْلَكَنِىَ ٱللَّهُ وَمَن مَّعِىَ
أَوْ رَحِمَنَا فَمَن يُجِيرُ ٱلْكَٰفِرِينَ مِنْ عَذَابٍ أَلِيمٍ ﴿٢٨﴾ قُلْ هُوَ
ٱلرَّحْمَٰنُ ءَامَنَّا بِهِۦ وَعَلَيْهِ تَوَكَّلْنَا ۖ فَسَتَعْلَمُونَ مَنْ هُوَ فِى ضَلَٰلٍ مُّبِينٍ
﴿٢٩﴾ قُلْ أَرَءَيْتُمْ إِنْ أَصْبَحَ مَآؤُكُمْ غَوْرًا فَمَن يَأْتِيكُم بِمَآءٍ مَّعِينٍۭ ﴿٣٠﴾

TRANSLATIONS

15. It is He, Who has made the earth manageable for you, so traverse you through its tracts and enjoy of the Sustenance which He furnishes: but unto Him is the Resurrection.

16. Do you feel secure that He Who is in Heaven will not cause you to be swallowed up by the earth when it shakes (as in an earthquake)?

17. Or do you feel secure that He Who is in Heaven will not send against you a violent tornado (with showers of stones),

15. He it is Who has made the earth subservient unto you, so walk in the paths thereof and eat of His providence. And unto Him will be the resurrection (of the dead).

16. Have you taken security from Him Who is in the heaven that He will not cause the earth to swallow you when lo! it is convulsed?

17. Or have you taken security from Him Who is in the heaven that He will not let loose on you a hurricane? But you shall

so that you shall know how (terrible) was My warning?

18. But indeed men before them rejected (My warning): then how (terrible) was My rejection (of them)?

19. Do they not observe the birds above them, spreading their wings and folding them in? None can uphold them except (Allāh) Most Gracious: truly it is He that watches over all things.

20. Nay, who is there that can help you, (even as) an army, besides (Allāh) Most Merciful? In nothing but delusion are the Unbelievers.

21. Or who is there that can provide you with Sustenance if He were to withhold His provision? Nay, they obstinately persist in insolent impiety and flight (from the Truth).

22. Is then one who walks headlong, with his face groveling, better guided or one who walks evenly on a Straight Way?

23. Say: "It is He Who has created you (and made you grow), and made for you the faculties of hearing, seeing, feeling and understanding: little thanks it is you give."

24. Say: "It is He Who has multiplied you through the earth, and to Him shall you be gathered together."

25. They ask: "When will this promise be (fulfilled)? If you are telling the truth."

26. Say: "As to the knowledge of the time, it is with Allāh alone: I am (sent) only to

know the manner of My warning.

18. And verily, those before them denied, then (see) the manner of My wrath (with them)!

19. Have they not seen the birds above them spreading out their wings and closing them? Naught upholds them save the Beneficent. Lo! He is Seer of all things.

20. Or who is he that will be an army unto you to help you instead of the Beneficent? The disbelievers are in naught but illusion.

21. Or who is he that will provide for you if He should withhold His providence? Nay, but they are set in pride and frowardness.

22. Is he who goes groping on his face more rightly guided, or he who walks upright on a beaten road?

23. Say (unto them, O Muhammad): He it is Who gave you being, and has assigned unto you ears and eyes and hearts. Small thanks give you!

24. Say: He it is Who multiplies you in the earth, and unto Whom you will be gathered.

25. And they say: When (will) this promise (be fulfilled), if you are truthful?

26. Say: The knowledge is with Allāh only, and I am but a plain warner;

warn plainly in public."

27. At length, when they see it close at hand, grieved will be the faces of the Unbelievers, and it will be said (to them): "This is (the promise fulfilled), which you were calling for!"

28. Say: "See you? - If Allāh were to destroy me, and those with me, or if He bestows His Mercy on us - yet who can deliver the Unbelievers from a grievous Penalty?"

29. Say: "He is (Allāh) Most Gracious: we have believed in Him, and on Him have we put our trust: so, soon will you know which (of us) it is that is in manifest error."

30. Say: "See you? - If your stream be some morning lost (in the underground earth), who then can supply you with clear-flowing water?"

(A. Y. Ali)

27. But when they see it nigh, the faces of those who disbelieve will be awry, and it will be said (unto them): This is that for which you used to call.

28. Say (O Muḥammad): Have you thought: Whether Allāh causes me (Muḥammad) and those with me to perish or has mercy on us, still, who will protect the disbelievers from a painful doom?

29. Say: He is the Beneficent. In Him we believe and in Him we put our trust. And you will soon know who it is that is in error manifest.

30. Say: Have you thought: If (all) your water were to disappear into the earth, who then could bring you gushing water?

(M. M. Pickthal)

EXPLANATION (A. Y. Ali, revised)

15: Humans have managed to make paths through deserts, mountains, rivers, seas, and air because Allāh سبحانه وتعالى has given them the necessary intelligence to do so, and He has made the earth obedient to that intelligence. In recognizing Allāh's gifts, it is clear that the ultimate end is the Hereafter.

16: If we feel safe on land, it is only because Allāh سبحانه وتعالى has made this earth amenable, manageable and serviceable to us. However, if we defy Allāh ﷻ and break His law, we have no security.

17-18: If we defy Allāh ﷻ and break His laws in this world, we have no security. How long will the temporary security granted by Allāh ﷻ last? The Qur'ān tells us about the People of `Ād and the nation of Thamūd and the community of Prophet Lūṭ ؑ, who were all destroyed because of their disobedience. We also know of the mighty men of the past: Pharaoh, Nimrod and Qarun; all of whom met a disgraceful death as a result of their continuous defiance of Allāh's commands. Their story is repeated throughout human history many times, warning us of the evil consequences of defiance. {See *al-Isrā'* 17:68; *al-`Ankabūt* 29:40, *al-Qaṣaṣ* 28:76-82 and *Al-Ḥajj* 22:42-44}

19: The flight of birds is one of the most beautiful and wondrous things in nature. It has inspired humans in the science and art of Aeronautics. But who taught birds this amazing ability? None but Allāh ﷻ Who, in His infinite Mercy and Wisdom, provides His creatures with conditions best adapted for their life on this earth.

20: Even the greatest {and most powerful} of armies that humans are able to organize is of no use against the Wrath of Allāh ﷻ. The constant, watchful care of Allāh ﷻ is our only protection, and we can never survive without it.

21: "Sustenance" refers to all that is necessary to support and develop life throughout all its stages, from birth until death. Allāh ﷻ, Most Gracious, is the only Source of all our sustenance. If we persist in looking elsewhere for our sustenance, we are following a path of rebellion and impiety.

22: The righteous person (*Muttaqī*) walks evenly on a Straight Way, his feet guided by Allāh's Light, and his heart sustained by Allāh's Mercy. The person who chooses evil walks fearfully, with his face turned downwards, in paths of darkness; stumbling all the way.

23: The Prophet ﷺ is reminded to draw constant attention to Allāh ﷻ, the Source of all growth and development; the Giver of the abilities by which we can judge right from wrong, and develop spiritually. And yet, such is our pride: we often use our faculties for wrong purposes, and thereby show our ingratitude to Allāh ﷻ.

24: From just one set of parents, humankind was multiplied and spread over the earth. We have not only multiplied in numbers, but we have also developed different languages and characteristics. Eventually, we will all be gathered together on the Day of Judgement, and the truth of Allāh ﷻ will rule over everyone.

25-26: The unbelievers are doubtful, but Judgement is certain to come. Only Allāh ﷻ knows when it will come exactly. The Prophet's duty is to proclaim that fact clearly. It is not for him to punish, or to hasten the punishment of evil.

27: "It" i.e., the fulfilment of the promise; the Day of Judgement. When it is actually in sight, it will become clearly evident that the faithful were right and that the sceptics were wrong. They asked for it. When it come near, and it becomes too late to change their ways, they will be weeping and regretful.

28: The skeptics, who are always doubtful, say to the righteous: "Ah well! If disasters come, it {always} involves good with the bad; just as you say that Allāh ﷻ showers His mercies on both good and evil!" The answer is: "Don't worry about us. Even if we are destroyed, will that be of any consolation to you? Your sins will surely bring suffering onto you, and nothing will ward it off. If we are struck with any sorrow or suffering, we take it as a mere trial, to make us better {stronger in our faith}. We believe in Allāh's Goodness, and we put our trust in Him."

29: Our faith tells us that Allāh ﷻ will save us from all harm if we sincerely change and begin to lead righteous lives and ask for forgiveness. The Unbelievers have no such hope.

30: The *Sūrah* closes with a parable that supports our physical life; it leads up to the understanding of our spiritual life. In our daily life, what would happen if we woke up one morning to find that the source of our water supply disappeared into the hollows of the earth? Nothing could save our lives.

Such is the spiritual life. Its sources are in the Divine wisdom that flows from Allāh ﷻ, the

Exalted. We must seek Allāh's ﷾ Grace and Mercy {to imporve} our spiritual life. We cannot find grace, mercy or blessing from anything lower.

IMPORTANT POINTS TO LEARN AND REFLECT UPON

- Allāh ﷾ has given us life, security, and provisions to enable us to live our lives comfortably.
- The righteous people walk steadfastly in His path, and the evil ones choose the crooked way of Satan.
- Allāh ﷾ is Most Gracious, and the believers place their complete trust in Him.

GLOSSARY WORDS

Traverse

VOCABULARY

بِسْمِ ٱللَّهِ ٱلرَّحْمَٰنِ ٱلرَّحِيمِ

الركوع ٢ - Section 2

(١٥) هُوَ الَّذِى	It is He Who	اَلنُّشُورُ	the Resurrection
جَعَلَ لَكُمُ ٱلْأَرْضَ	has made the earth for you	(١٦) ءَأَمِنْتُمْ	Do you feel secure
ذَلُولاً	manageable, obedient	مَّنْ فِى السَّمَآءِ	that He Who is in heaven
فَامْشُوا	so you walk	أَنْ يَّخْسِفَ	cause you to be swallowed up
فِى مَنَاكِبِهَا	its tracts	بِكُمُ ٱلْأَرْضَ	by the earth
وَكُلُوا مِنْ رِزْقِهِ	and eat of His sustenance	فَإِذَا هِىَ تَمُورُ	when it shakes
وَ إِلَيْهِ	and unto Him is	(١٧) أَمْ أَمِنْتُمْ	Or do you feel secure
		مَّنْ فِى السَّمَآءِ	He Who is in heaven

أَنْ يُرْسِلَ عَلَيْكُمْ	will not send against you
حَاصِبًا	a violent tornado
فَسَتَعْلَمُونَ	so that you shall know
كَيْفَ نَذِيرِ	how terrible was My warning
(١٨) وَ لَقَدْ كَذَّبَ	But indeed rejected
الَّذِينَ مِنْ قَبْلِهِمْ	those before them
فَكَيْفَ كَانَ نَكِيرِ	then how was My rejection
(١٩) أَوَلَمْ يَرَوْا	Do they not observe
إِلَى الطَّيْرِ فَوْقَهُمْ	the birds above them
صَٰفَّٰتٍ	spreading their wings
وَ يَقْبِضْنَ	and folding
مَا يُمْسِكُهُنَّ	none can uphold them
إِلَّا الرَّحْمَٰنُ	except the Most Gracious
إِنَّهُ	truly it is He
بِكُلِّ شَيْءٍ بَصِيرٌ	over all things that Watches
(٢٠) أَمَّنْ هَٰذَا الَّذِى	Nay, who is there
هُوَ جُنْدٌ لَّكُمْ	an army for you
يَنْصُرُكُمْ	can help you
مِّنْ دُونِ الرَّحْمَٰنِ	besides the Most Merciful
إِنِ الْكَٰفِرُونَ	indeed the unbelievers
إِلَّا فِى غُرُورٍ	in nothing but pride

(٢١) أَمَّنْ هَٰذَا الَّذِى	Or who is there
يَرْزُقُكُمْ	to provide you
إِنْ أَمْسَكَ	if He were to withhold
رِزْقَهُ	His provision
بَل لَّجُّوا	nay they persist
فِى عُتُوٍّ	in insolent impiety
وَّ نُفُورٍ	and flight (from the truth)
(٢٢) أَفَمَنْ يَمْشِى	Is then one who walks
مُكِبًّا	headlong with
عَلَىٰ وَجْهِهِ	with his face grovelling
أَهْدَىٰ	better guided
أَمَّنْ يَمْشِى	or one who walks
سَوِيًّا	evenly
عَلَىٰ صِرَاطٍ مُّسْتَقِيمٍ	on a Straight Way
(٢٣) قُلْ هُوَ الَّذِى	Say: It is He Who
أَنْشَأَكُمْ	has created you
وَجَعَلَ لَكُمُ	and made for you
السَّمْعَ	the faculty of hearing
وَ الْأَبْصَارَ	and seeing
وَ الْأَفْئِدَةَ	and understanding
قَلِيلًا مَّا تَشْكُرُونَ	little thanks it is you give

(٢٤) قُلْ هُوَ الَّذِى	Say: It is He Who	تَدَّعُونَ	calling for
ذَرَأَكُمْ	has multiplied you	(٢٨) قُلْ أَرَءَيْتُمْ	Say: See you
فِى الْأَرْضِ	through the earth	إِنْ أَهْلَكَنِىَ اللهُ	if Allah were to destroy me
وَ إِلَيْهِ	and to Him	وَمَنْ مَّعِىَ	and those with me
تُحْشَرُونَ	shall you be gathered together	أَوْ رَحِمَنَا	or He has His Mercy on us
(٢٥) وَيَقُولُونَ	And they ask	فَمَنْ يُجِيرُ	yet who can deliver
مَتَىٰ هٰذَا	when will this	الْكٰفِرِينَ	the unbelievers
الْوَعْدُ	promise (be fulfilled)	مِنْ عَذَابٍ أَلِيمٍ	from a grievous penalty
إِنْ كُنْتُمْ صٰدِقِينَ	if you are telling the truth	(٢٩) قُلْ هُوَ	Say: He is (Allah)
(٢٦) قُلْ إِنَّمَا	Say: As to	الرَّحْمٰنُ	the Most Gracious
الْعِلْمُ	the knowledge (of its time)	ءَامَنَّا بِهِ	we have believed in Him
عِنْدَ اللهِ	it is with Allah (alone)	وَعَلَيْهِ	and on Him
وَ إِنَّمَآ أَنَا	and I am only	تَوَكَّلْنَا	put our trust
نَذِيرٌ مُّبِينٌ	a plain warner	فَسَتَعْلَمُونَ	so, soon will you know
(٢٧) فَلَمَّا رَأَوْهُ	At length, when they see	مَنْ هُوَ	which (of us) it is
زُلْفَةً	close at hand	فِى ضَلٰلٍ مُّبِينٍ	that is in manifest error
سِيٓـَٔتْ	grieved will be	(٣٠) قُلْ أَرَءَيْتُمْ	Say: See you
وُجُوهُ الَّذِينَ	the faces of those who	إِنْ أَصْبَحَ	if becomes one morning
كَفَرُوا	disbelieved	مَآؤُكُمْ غَوْرًا	your water (stream) lost
وَقِيلَ هٰذَا الَّذِى	and it will be said this is	فَمَنْ يَأْتِيكُمْ	who then can supply you
كُنْتُمْ بِهِ	which you were	بِمَآءٍ مَّعِينٍ	with clear, flowing water

Section 1:1-3

سُورَةُ العَصْرِ

SŪRAH AL-‘AṢR 103: 1-3

The Through The Ages / The Declining Day

Name: This *Sūrah* is named after the first word, *al-`Aṣr*, of the first verse. *Al-`Aṣr* has two meanings: time in general, and the time of the declining day (the time of *Ṣalāt al-Aṣr*).

Period of Revelation: Some traditions consider it a Madīnan *Sūrah*, but the majority of the commentators regard it as Makkan. Both its style and teachings clearly suggest that it is an early Makkan *Sūrah*.

Theme and Subject Matter: This *Sūrah* is brief, yet full of meaning. Its three short verses offer a commentary on the human experience of loss with the (inevitable) passage of time. It also prescribes a formula to ensure success in both worlds.

It is related by bin Hisn ad-Darimi Abu Madīnah ﵁ that whenever any two of the *Ṣaḥābah* met, they would not depart from one another's company until they recited *Sūrah Al-Aṣr* to each other. (Tabarāni)

ARABIC TEXT

بِسْمِ اللَّهِ الرَّحْمَٰنِ الرَّحِيمِ

وَالْعَصْرِ ﴿١﴾ إِنَّ الْإِنسَانَ لَفِي خُسْرٍ ﴿٢﴾ إِلَّا الَّذِينَ آمَنُوا
وَعَمِلُوا الصَّالِحَاتِ وَتَوَاصَوْا بِالْحَقِّ وَتَوَاصَوْا بِالصَّبْرِ ﴿٣﴾

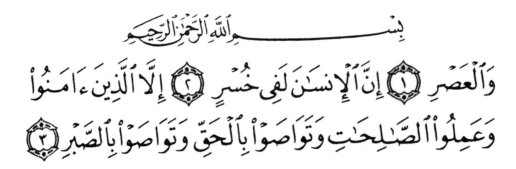

TRANSLATIONS

1. By (the Token of) time (through the Ages) {*Wa (a)l-'Aṣr*},

2. Verily Human is in loss,

3. Except such as have Faith, and do righteous deeds, and (join together) in the mutual teaching {*Tawāṣaw*) of Truth {*al-Ḥaqq*}, and of Patience and Constancy {*aṣ-Ṣabr*}.

(A. Y. Ali)

1. By the declining day,

2. Lo! man is in a state of loss,

3. Save those who believe and do good works, and exhort one another to truth and exhort one another to endurance.

(M. M. Pickthal)

EXPLANATION (A. Y. Ali, revised)

1: *Al-`Aṣr* means:

(1) Time through the Ages

(2) or the late afternoon, from which the *`Aṣr* prayer takes its name.

An appeal is made {to mankind} using Time as one of the creations of Allāh سبحانه وتعالى. Time searches out and destroys material things. If we attempt to run a race against time, we shall {certainly} lose. It is only the spiritual part of us that conquers time.

2: If life is considered a trade {*Tijārah*}, every human will lose. When he makes up his day's account in the afternoon, it will show a loss. It will only show profit if he has faith, leads a good life, and contributes to social welfare by encouraging other people to follow the path of truth (*al-Ḥaqq*) and constancy (*as-Ṣabr*).

3: Faith is a believer's armor. It protects him from the wounds of the material world, and his righteous life is a positive contribution to his spiritual ascent. If the believer lived only for himself, he would not fulfill his duty. Whatever good he has, especially in terms of his moral and spiritual life, he must spread it among humanity. He must make others see the truth (*al-Ḥaqq*), and stand by that truth in patient hope (*as-Ṣabr*) and unshaken constancy (*Tawāṣaw*), amid all the storms and stresses of his life. Only then will he have attained inner peace and true success in the Hereafter.

IMPORTANT POINTS TO LEARN AND REFLECT UPON

- Time is a witness to human suffering and loss.
- Only the believers with right actions escape this loss.
- It is not sufficient to believe oneself, but we must share the Truth with others with patience and constancy.

GLOSSARY WORDS

al-`Aṣr, al-Ḥaqq, aṣ-Ṣabr, Tawāṣ aw

VOCABULARY

سورة العصر - ٣٢

الركوع ١ - Section 1

بِسْمِ اللهِ الرَّحْمٰنِ الرَّحِيمِ

(١) وَ الْعَصْرِ	By the time	اَلصّٰلِحٰتِ	good
(٢) إِنَّ الْإِنْسَانَ	Surely human	وَ تَوَصَوْا	and exhort
لَفِى خُسْرٍ	is in loss	بِالْحَقِّ	one another to truth
(٣) إِلاَّ الَّذِينَ	Except those who	وَ تَوَاصَوْا	and exhort
اٰمَنُوا	believe	بِالصَّبْرِ	one another to patience
وَعَمِلُوا	and do		

Glossary

Cherisher	The one who treats with tenderness and affection; who fosters; who nurtures
Consequence	A logical result or conclusion
Conviction	Strong belief
Credential	To believe, put trust in
Degradation	The act of depriving one of a degree of honor dignity, or rank
Deterioration	Worse; of lower value, quality
Disgrace	To put out of favor, to bring shame or dishonor upon
Disharmony	Absence of harmony, discord
Estuaries	Inlets or arms of the sea; wide mouths of a river
Faculties	Any natural or specialized power of a living organism
Grace	Beauty or charm of form, composition, movement, or expression
Grasp	To seize and hold by clasping or embracing with the fingers or arms; to seize mentally to understand
Grossness	The quality of being gross; the total amount
Harmony	A combination of parts into an orderly or proportionate whole
Lunar	Of or having to do with the moon
Mingle	To be or become mixed, combined

Obstinacy	The quality of being obstinate, to set one's mind firmly on
Omen	A thing or occurrence thought to predict good or evil
Parable	A short, simple story from which a moral lesson may be drawn
Rebellion	An act or state of open resistance to authority
Repentance	The state of being feeling sorrow or regret for what has been done
Righteous	Acting in a just, upright manner
Similitude	A person or thing resembling another
Solar	Of or having to do with the sun
Transformation	The act or operation of changing the form or external appearance
Traverse	To pass over; to across

IQRA'
TRANSLITERATION CHART

q	ق	*	z	ز		'	أء	*
k	ك		s	س		b	ب	
l	ل		<u>sh</u>	ش		t	ت	
m	م		ṣ	ص	*	<u>th</u>	ث	*
n	ن		ḍ	ض	*	j	ج	
h	هـ		ṭ	ط	*	ḥ	ح	*
w	و		ẓ	ظ	*	<u>kh</u>	خ	*
y	ي		‘	ع	*	d	د	
			<u>gh</u>	غ	*	<u>dh</u>	ذ	*
			f	ف		r	ر	

SHORT VOWELS	LONG VOWELS	DIPHTHONGS
a \ ـَـ	ā \ ـَا	aw \ ـَوْ
u \ ـُـ	ū \ ـُو	ai \ ـَيْ
i \ ـِـ	ī \ ـِي	
Such as: *kataba* كَتَبَ	Such as: *Kitāb* كِتَاب	Such as: *Lawh* لَوْح
Such as: *Qul* قُلْ	Such as: *Mamnūn* مَمْنُون	Such as: *'Ain* عَيْن
Such as: *Ni'mah* نِعْمَة	Such as: *Dīn* دِين	

* Special attention should be given to the symbols marked with stars for they have no equivalent in the English sounds .

Note : Letters in parenthesis (a),(i),(u) appear in writing but are not pronounced.

ISLAMIC INVOCATIONS:

Rasūlullāh, *Ṣalla Allahu ʻalaihi wa Sallam* (صَلَّى ٱللَّهُ عَلَيْهِ وَسَلَّم), and the Qur'ān teaches us to glorify Allāh ﷻ when we mention His Name and to invoke His Blessings when we mention the names of His Angels, Messengers, the *Ṣaḥābah* and the Pious Ancestors.

When we mention the Name of Allāh we must say: *Subḥāna-hū Wa-Taʻālā* (سُبْحَانَهُ وَتَعَالَى), Glorified is He and High. In this book we write ﷻ to remind ourselves to glorify Allāh.

When we mention the name of Rasūlullāh ﷺ we must say: *Ṣalla Allāhu ʻalai-hi wa-Sallam,* (صَلَّى ٱللَّهُ عَلَيْهِ وَسَلَّم), May Allāh's Blessings and Peace be upon him.
We write ﷺ to remind ourselves to invoke Allāh's Blessings on Rasūlullāh.

When we mention the name of an angel or a prophet we must say: *Alai-hi-(a)s-Salām* (عَلَيْهِ ٱلسَّلَام), Upon him be peace.
We write ؑ to remind ourselves to invoke Allāh's Peace upon him.

When we hear the name of the *Ṣaḥābah* we must say:
For a *Ṣaḥābī*, *Raḍiya-(A)llāhu Taʻālā ʻan-hu* (رَضِيَ ٱللَّهُ تَعَالَى عَنْهُ), May Allāh be pleased with him.
We write ؓ to remind ourselves to invoke Allah's pleasure on them.

For more than two, *Raḍiya-(A)llāhu Taʻālā ʻan-hum,* (رَضِيَ ٱللَّهُ تَعَالَى عَنْهُم), May Allāh be pleased with them.
We write ؓ to remind ourselves to invoke Allah's pleasure on them.

For a *Ṣaḥābiyyah*, *Raḍiya-(A)llāhu Taʻālā ʻan-hā* (رَضِيَ ٱللَّهُ تَعَالَى عَنْهَا), May Allāh be pleased with her.
We write ؓ to remind ourselves to invoke Allah's pleasure on her.

For two of them, *Raḍiya-(A)llāhu Taʻālā ʻan-humā* (رَضِيَ ٱللَّهُ تَعَالَى عَنْهُمَا), May Allāh be pleased with both of them.
We write ؓ to remind ourselves to invoke Allah's pleasure on them.

When we hear the name of the Pious Ancestor *(As-Salaf aṣ-Ṣāliḥ)* we must say:
For a man, *Raḥmatu-(A)llāh ʻalai-hi* (رَحْمَةُ ٱللَّهِ عَلَيْهِ), May Allāh's Mercy be upon him.
For a woman, *Raḥmatu-(A)llāh ʻalai-hā* (رَحْمَةُ ٱللَّهِ عَلَيْهَا), May Allāh's Mercy be with her.

INTRODUCING THE AUTHOR

Dr. Abidullah Ghazi, Executive Director of IQRA' International, and his wife, Dr. Tasneema Ghazi, Director of Curriculum, are co–founders of IQRA' International Educational Foundation (a non–profit Islamic educational trust) and Chief Editors of its educational program. They have combined their talents and expertise and dedicated their lives to produce a Comprehensive Program of Islamic Studies for our children and youth and to develop IQRA' into a major center of research and development for Islamic Studies, specializing in Islamic education.

Abidullah Ghazi, M. A. (Alig), M. Sc. Econ. (LSE London), Ph. D. (Harvard)

Dr. Abidullah Ghazi, a specialist in Islamic Studies and Comparative Religion, belongs to a prominent family of the Ulama' of India. His family has been active in the field of Islamic education, *dawah*, and struggle for freedom. Dr. Ghazi's early education was carried in traditional *Madaris.* He later studied at Muslim University, Aligarh, The London School of Economics, and Harvard University. He has taught at the Universities of Jamia Millia Islamia, Delhi, London, Harvard, San Diego, Minnesota, Northwestern, Governors State and King Abdul Aziz, Jeddah. He is a consultant for the development of the program of Islamic Studies in various schools and universities. He is a well–known community worker, speaker, writer and poet.